Captain John Norwood V.C.

A Man of Kent

Prologue

Captain John Norwood V.C.

The Rugby School register has the following entry for John Norwood.

"J Norwood was the only son of John and Lucy Norwood of Pembury Lodge, New Beckenham Kent. He entered Rugby in 1891, was in the shooting eight that won the Ashburton Shield at Bisley in 1894. In the same year he went up to Exeter College Oxford. He received his Commission as a university candidate in the 5th Dragoon Guards in 1899. He went to India in the same year and to South Africa at the outbreak of the Boer War. He was present at the battle of Elandslagte (October 21 1899) and on the eve of the battle of Lombards Kop (October 31), in which he took part, performed the act for which he was subsequently given the VC. He served throughout the siege of Ladysmith, during which he was attacked by enteric fever. After a short interval, he returned to South Africa, and remained in active service until the end of the war. For his service, he received the Queen's Medal with four clasps and the King's medal with two.

Between 1902 and 1909 he served in England, India South Africa and Dublin and then left the Army. He was offered the post of King's Messenger but was unable to accept it. After he left the Army, he was keenly interested in everything connected with it. In the course of a busy life, he found time to organise and work with the Old Comrades Association in connection with his old regiment. He trained annually with the Territorials and at the outbreak of war was attached to the Westminster Dragoons. He worked hard to get them ready, but, at the request of the Colonel then commanding the 5th Dragoon Guards, he rejoined his old regiment and left for France on August 15 1914.

He was in the retreat from Mons and in the advance to the Marne. On his 38th birthday, September 8th 1914, he was given his company Squadron. On that day a half Squadron of the 5th Dragoon Guards was acting as an advance guard, and had reached the bank of the Petit Morin River near Sablonnieres, when it came under heavy fire. One of his sergeants was wounded, and Captain Norwood managed to reach him and bind him up. He was trying to reach the horses left in the rear when he was shot and died instantly, aged 38.

He married in 1904, Lilian, only daughter of Major General Sir

Edwin Collen, KCIE, CB and left two sons and one daughter."

This memoir about the life of John Norwood V.C. originated from reading his diaries which covered his youthful expedition to the foothills of the Himalayas and his engagement in the Anglo South African war, in the course of which he won the Victoria Cross. There are also letters from France to his wife during the approach to Mons, the retreat and then the advance to the Marne where he became the first V.C. to die in the war. It is clear from these pages that although he was in many respects an ebullient, headstrong Cavalry officer of the kind that emerges frequently from the pages of late Victorian romantic fiction, a man whom readers of the novels of Rider Haggard would have appreciated, he was kind and considerate. This aspect of him is seen not only in letters to his children and wife, but also in the obituaries which appeared after his death. When I mentioned his name many years ago   to the distinguished military historian Richard Holmes, now sadly deceased, to my great surprise he immediately quoted from memory several letters which had been deposited in the Imperial War Museum that he had seen before writing his book "Riding the Retreat". Richard shared my admiration for him.

John came from a well-established line of Kent knights, squires and yeomen going back to the Conquest. There had been no recent association with the Army however other than his great grandparent's participation in the Queen's Own West Kent Yeomanry which was a volunteer Cavalry Regiment of the British Army, first raised in 1794 to defend the United Kingdom against invasion by the French during the Napoleonic Wars. Each troop had been about 50 strong with three officers (Captain, Lieutenant, Cornet); they were required to provide their own uniforms and mounts while the government would supply their arms and ammunition. It is doubtful that this connection had much to do with John's later decision to seek a commission. However his marriage to the daughter of General Edwin Collen brought him mainstream military connections, including with his brother in law Lieutenant Colonel Edward Collen RA, who participated in frontier campaigns in India, the Boer War and the First World and whose diaries have also contributed to this story.

Whilst General Collen's rise to the top of the Indian Army to become the Military Member on the Viceroy's Council was due very much in the second half of his career to his administrative skills, he had enjoyed lively experiences in Africa in the campaign to release European hostages from the Ethiopian Emperor Theodore in 1868 and also in the East Sudan expedition of 1885 based in Suakin as part of the ill-fated effort to relieve General Gordon in Khartoum. Later he survived Maiwand, a serious British defeat, in the Second Afghan War. In many respects therefore, John's military career was a progression from that of his future father in law. John's regiment the 5th Dragoons played an important part in the Nile campaign to save Gordon and it also had elements in the frontier campaign, including the containment of the Afridi in the Tyrah war. I have sought to weave all of these elements into John's story.

It has been helpful in recording the war experiences laid out in the book that I have visited practically all of the sites concerned, from Ethiopia, upon which I have not dwelt, through Suakin in Eastern Sudan (now a fascinating ruin after earthquake damage) to the Anglo South African war battlefields. Visiting the Tamai battlefield where the British square was broken with the Governor of the Eastern Province was particularly memorable. I recall that we stood together in the desert on the back of a Land Rover trying to make sense of the fighting, looking towards the wadi from which the Mahdists had struck. I gave my best interpretation of what had happened to his staff, standing alongside the ancient obelisk erected by the British marking the battlefield. I gave the Governor a copy of the key book on this subject, Brian Robson's "Fuzzy-Wuzzy: the campaigns in the Eastern Sudan 1884-8", conscious of the potentially pejorative overtones of the words "Fuzzy Wuzzy" and the possibility that he might take offence. However the modern descendants of the Hadendowa regard the term with pride, perhaps because Kipling's quote helped anchor their important place in history.

I have also visited General Collen's rather grand home in Shimla (which is now a major Art gallery and his more modest one in Kelvedon (formerly the Bell Inn). His obituaries place him firmly in that pantheon, now forgotten, of historical figures to whom the British Empire owed a great deal and who retired afterwards to a modest life in the Home Counties.

I had an additional reason for interest in the Boer war operations because my own grandfather was in the Second Battalion of the Gloucester Regiment and served in the Orange River Colony and the Transvaal. He was wounded and taken prisoner at Dewetsdorp and subsequently invalided out of the Army traumatized by his experiences. His sister unit, the First Battalion, had been with John Norwood in Ladysmith and indeed John was trying to find out what had happened to them in their disastrous night operation at Nicholson's Nek when he won his Victoria Cross. Furthermore, my father was a reservist who was called up into the British Expeditionary Force in August 1914, participated in the Battle of Mons, then the retreat to Paris before going forward to the Chemin des Dames with his Regiment, the Second Battalion of the Welch. He marched closely on John's heels at Sablonierres where John was killed, and then survived a year on the Western Front before being repatriated to the UK with enteric fever in September 1915.

I am indebted to the pioneering war artist Melton Prior for his stirring accounts of the Nile campaign drawn from his memoirs which were published by the US Library of Congress in the interests of historical journalism. His assignments for the Illustrated London News for which he drew war sketches are a roll call of late Victorian military history. He took exactly the same risks as his military colleagues but miraculously survived when some of his journalist colleagues joined the fallen. He was in Ladysmith with the British Force and memorably sketched John's V.C. action. Prior lived and died not a mile from my home. His sketch of John is now on loan from the family to the Royal Dragoon Guards Museum in York. Many of John's photographs of the Boer War are in the archives of the National Army Museum and his medals are on long term loan to the VC and GC collection of the Imperial war Museum.

A common characteristic of the colonial wars in Africa and especially in Afghanistan and on the North West frontier was that the enemy gave no quarter and expected none. These were not battles in which mercy was shown to the captured and wounded as far as the opponent was concerned. In the East Sudan campaign whilst the British initially respected the rules of war, they soon found that a badly wounded Mahdist would seek to stab his opponent even from the ground rather than receive such basic help as water. The consequence was inevitable - few prisoners were taken. The effect of this kind of warfare on the minds of soldiers recruited from the county regiments like the Gloucesters, the Middlesex and Sussex Regiments, as well as Scots regiments like the Black Watch can only be imagined.

Conversely, the rules of war in the Anglo South African campaign were almost gentlemanly - at the siege of Ladysmith, the Boers allowed the hospital at Intombi where John Norwood was treated for enteric fever to be regarded as neutral territory, free from bombardment or military action. There were many deaths at Intombi due to inadequate treatment, and the limitations of medical knowledge at the time, notably the absence of antibiotics and poor infection control. The outlook for men wounded and treated in the field on any battle field in the 19th century was dire. Enteric fever still claimed many victims in the First World War even after repatriation from the western front to the UK.

John left a very young family behind when he died in 1914 but the tradition of service which his life encapsulated was carried on into the Second World War where all three of his children served with distinction in various aspects of the defence of Britain. Sadly, Lilian Blanche Norwood nee Collen died in 1937 in London after a long widowhood. My wife Gay is amongst the five grandchildren of Lilian and John.

Chapter 1

Medieval History of the Norwood

The Norwood family were men of Kent whose ancestry has been traced back to the marriage of Harold Godwinson also known as Harold II, the last king of Anglo-Saxon England, and his wife Edith Swannaschels (known as Swans-neck) and their eldest son Alnod, frequently referred to in the Domesday Book and other accounts as Alnod, Cilt and occasionally Ulf. He was placed by his father in a position of power (probably Sheriff) at an early age. Before the Conquest, Alnod had held twenty Kentish Manors, but at the time of the Domesday survey, he had lost all of his holdings. He is believed to be the young man in the scene with Harold recording his encounter with Edward in the opening part of the Bayeux tapestry and later with Harold when he arrived at William's palace. Harold lost his throne of course at Hastings in 1066.

The lands held by Alnod were conveyed to William the Conqueror's brother Odo, Bishop of Bayeux after Hastings. The area covered by this holding stretched from the hilltop on the Isle of Sheppey, across what is now flat grazing marshland, over the River Swale to the mainland beyond Milton. After the death of William the Conqueror in 1087, his successor William Rufus, having no more to fear from the sons of Harold, released Alnod who also benefitted from the favour of Robert Curthose, the contentious second son of William the Conqueror who was always at odds with his father.

Three years after the death of William in 1087, the First Crusade to recover the Holy Land from the Turks engaged the attention of Europe. Although Alnod himself did not take part

in the Crusades, it has been stated that through the influence of these holy pilgrimages, he changed his name to Jordanus. The Christian name "Jordanus" was unusual at this early period, and normally would be adopted only by one who had taken a religious pilgrimage to the Holy Land, and received baptism in the river Jordan. More practically, Alnod seized by force two parts of the King's Wood at Milton, which he was later permitted to hold, as he had before the Conquest, not by feudal but by customary tenure, and he then lived high on the Sheppey hilltop overlooking this land. Both Alnod and Edith Swannaschels, who had taken refuge in Sheppey after her husband's death, are buried in unmarked graves in Minster Abbey, although a large stone recovered by archaeologists in recent times may well be his tomb marker. Edith died in 1086. The building on Sheppey now called Norwood Manor, first known as Northwood Manor, was built in 1126 and remained a feature of the local landscape until it was destroyed in Cromwell's time, resulting in the building of the present manor house in about 1670.

There is some debate about the chronology of the link between Alnod and Stephen de Northwood. As Alnod is believed to have been born in 1042 and it would be unusual for him to sire Stephen in extreme old age. It is more likely that the latter, born in 1125 was his grandson. This detail is likely to be long argued and is incapable of proof. Stephen joined the Third Crusade (1189-1192) with King Richard 1, known as Coeur de Lion, and took the name Northwood from the position of the wooded lands he held in the parish of Milton, and thereafter his Manor was known as Northwood without Sheppey to distinguish it from that of his father, known as Northwood within Sheppey. Additional evidence for the Alnod-Norwood connection comes from the historian Henry Bracton (1210-1268), an English cleric and jurist and a contemporary of Roger de Northwood in the reign of Henry III who describes Roger's lands as descending from his ancestor Alnod. Bracton is famous now for his writings on law but he also wrote on kingship.

Stephen was knighted by Richard I in 1191 after the battle of Acre. He was now an eminent man, celebrating by building the chapel of Newington Church, according to the framed inscription in that church. He resided at Northwood now called Norwood in Bobbing, where he had a moated mansion, the remains of the moat being still visible today. He also owned some land in the eastern part of the parish of Newington, his coat of arms being formerly in the windows of Newington Church. There is high up in the chapel at Holy Trinity Milton Regis (which was again built by the Northwoods in their pomp in the 15th century) a wooden replica of a helmet called the" Northwood Helm", the original of which resides in the Tower Armory in London.

Considerable damage had been inflicted on Minster Abbey during earlier Viking and then the Norman invasions. The Saxons of Sheppey had not welcomed the Normans arrival and their resistance exacted a toll before they were persuaded to lay down their arms. Finally, Henry 1 visited the island and gave instructions for repairs to be undertaken. Sir Stephen's son Sir Roger de Northwood and his consort, Lady Bona Fitzbernard became major benefactors of the reconstruction and when he died in 1286 he was buried in the Abbey Church. He was steward of the Archbishop of Canterbury's lands from 1258 to 1274 when he became Baron of the Exchequer. He served as Warden of the Cinque Ports in 1257 and as a Justice in Kent, serving on various judicial commissions.

The earliest lists of those who were entitled to bear arms were known as Rolls of Arms. The first of these Rolls was inscribed on a long narrow parchment in 1240, now preserved in the British Museum. The Roll of Caerlaverock, dated 1300, registers those knights and nobles present with Edward I at the Siege of Caerlaverock Castle in Dumfries, Scotland, together with their coats of arms. On this roll is the name of Sir Roger's son, Sir John de Northwood, (who married Lady Joan de Badlesmere) who was knighted by Edward I after the battle. His neighbour, Robert de Shurland was knighted during the same campaign.

King John of Scotland's reign ended in 1296 when Edward I of England invaded Scotland. The invasion caused many Scots to swear loyalty to Edward I, among them being Herbert Maxwell and his son John. When the Scots still resisted and the Maxwells reneged on their oath, Edward I came back to Scotland in 1300 and invaded Galloway, one of the strongest areas of resistance. Caerlaverock Castle, the Maxwell's base, overlooking the Solway Firth was a prime target. Edward brought 87 knights and 3,000 men to Caerlaverock. The garrison could only withstand 2 days of pummelling and thanks to a detailed account of the battle from a herald in Edward's Army; this became one of the best known military operations of the Wars. The defenders were hanged from the battlements.

By the medieval period, the right to use a coat of arms had to be granted by the Sovereign, and in 1413 the Heralds Visitations were established to give authority to those legally entitled to bear arms. It is from these sources, the Rolls of Arms and Herald's Visitations, that the early coats of arms of the Norwood family can be known with a high degree of authority. Sir John was an active military campaigner. He fought in France in 1294, in Flanders in in 1297 and five times in Scotland between 1309 and 1318. He was summoned to the Coronation of Edward 11 in 1308 and entered Parliament as Baron Northwood, being styled as one of the "Great Barons". He and his wife died in in 1319.

There are splendid Norwood brasses for Sir John and his wife in the Abbey Church of Minister which date from about 1320. The Whipple or headdress which forms part of the costume of the lady was allowed to be worn only by ladies of title, and the way it was put on indicated the rank of the wearer. As represented on the engraving on the brasses, it shows that Sir John's wife was a nobleman's daughter and a lady in her own right. If she had been a princess, it would have been worn high enough to hide her lips. If she were merely a knight's wife it would have reached her chin. The crossed legs as seen on Sir John meant that he fought in the crusades. The animals behind the feet were symbolic, too.

A dog (as found behind Lady Joan's feet) meant that the person had died a peaceful, natural death. The small lion, as found behind Sir John's feet symbolized a violent death as in battle.

Sir John's son, also called John, lived from 1279 to 1320 and married Lady Agnes de Grandison of Ottery St Mary whose own descent came from Lord Tregoz, a Norman knight who stood alongside William at Hastings. By this time, the Norwood association with the Anglo Saxon Jordanus and Harold had long disappeared discreetly from sight! The couple's eldest son, Sir Roger (1307-61) must have been a hard driving spouse as he managed to get through 5 marriages. The Dane Court and thence Stilstead line of the Norwoods is thought to descend from Sir Roger de Northwood's third marriage to Margery de Halglton, who was a widow bringing with her into the family a daughter Margaret. The latter then proceeded to marry Sir Roger's son, her step brother, also called Sir Richard, which is quite confusing. She thereby became both a stepdaughter and daughter in law to Sir Roger! Conversation must have been somewhat incestuous around the banqueting table.

Sir Roger continued the tradition of knightly service; he was called to fight in Scotland in 1334 and 5 years later, he was chief of those appointed to provide for the defence of the Kent coast from invasion. He was summoned to Parliament in1360. His son John, who died in 1379, served in France, was regularly called to Parliament and in 1369 was sent to Sheppey to defend it against possible French invasion. His son Roger engaged in similar duties but the Barony of Northwood fell vacant because Sir John de Northwood of the next generation died without heirs in 1416.

There is a final glorious funerary spasm of the Norwood family however which can be seen at Holy Trinity Milton Regis. Three generations beyond the death of Sir John, Norwood without Sheppey (also known as Norwood Chasteners), passes out of the hands of the Norwood family when it is given as a dowry by her father John to Joan de Northwood, (born 1491) when she married Sir John Norton. Their joint magnificent tomb is in the chapel of the church. Sir John Norton was Sheriff of Kent in 1514 and died in 1534. His knighthood was gained in the Low Countries and was conferred on him by Charles King of Castile. Their son, who became Sir John Norton de Northwood was knighted in 1546 and was present at the funeral of Henry VIII.

The Northwood Chantry chapel containing the tomb and coats of arms of both the Norwoods and the Nortons was added to the church in about 1450. There are also brasses dated from 1496 of Sir John and Joan.

Chapter 2

The Thanet Norwoods

There can be no doubt of the distinction and importance of the medieval baronial family of Northwood. It is the connection between this family, linked to Milton Regis and the Norwoods of Thanet that is more conjectural and which needs further examination in the context of the Dane Court family.

Marian Norwood Callum has used direct genealogical descent to connect the Thanet Norwoods with Milton Regis and has postulated a series of plausible connections but there is a lack of documentary evidence to underpin her proposition, although it has a high level of credibility. The simple facts are that we know very little about the next three generations of Norwoods, starting with Thomas de Northwood (born 1350), considered to be the son of Sir Roger de Northwood and Margaret de Halglton, his son Richard (1374) his grandson, Thomas (1396) and great grandson Richard (1420-85). The similarity of the various coats of arms used by the families concerned as well as the common names are also attested as evidence. The debate between genealogists can become quite abstruse. It is clear that when Manassas Norwood bought the old Manor of Norwood Chasteners and had ancient shields carved on his tomb, he was anxious to strengthen his association with the Milton Barons probably because he believed the association to be true. There is an historic connection in the sense at the very least that members of the Thanet line acted as if they were so descended by using the arms of their Milton namesake. It is unlikely that hard evidence will emerge now to settle the discussion.

The Norwood clearly prospered under their crest of a Boar's Head and in 1441 at least four Norwood connections held lands in Thanet. They lived however through turbulent times. The Black Death arrived from the continent in the summer of 1348 killing around 40% of the British population and wiping out many villages. Peasants from Kent formed the majority of Wat Tyler's force when in 1381 they marched from Canterbury to London and held King Richard II in thrall until Tyler, who was born in the county, after rallying his forces on Blackheath, was killed by one of the Kings retainers, thus decapitating the rising. Their grievance was heavy taxation and an unpopular government. The term "Peasants" Revolt is somewhat misleading as many of the men who were to take up arms that summer were far from what we would think of as peasants today. Many were from the yeoman classes, skilled men and village leaders. Their fight wasn't against misery, hunger or poverty, instead it was a call for liberty, justice and an end to the feudal system that still kept many free born Englishmen as mere slaves to the lords of the manor. It was a moral crusade for emancipation and for what they believed to be right.

Another peasant leader from Kent, Jack Cade raised both the peasantry and the gentry, including clergy, on similar grounds in 1450 before he was killed in his turn. The rebellion was an uprising against the policies of Henry VI. The majority of the participants were peasants and small landowners from Kent, who objected to forced labour, corrupt courts, the seizure of land by nobles, the loss of royal lands in France, and heavy taxation. As if these troubles were not enough, in the 15th century, the country was roiled by the Wars of the Roses between the contending Yorkist and Lancastrian branches of the royal family from 1453 to 1458 which touched all sectors of society.

Overseas, the Hundred Years war between England and France began in 1337 and lead to some legendary engagements. According to local history, Thomas de Northwood of Milton, entertained at a cost of nine shillings and nine pence King Henry V and his entourage on his return from the Battle of Agincourt in November 1415 at the Red Lion in Sittingbourne, not yet aware perhaps that he would be dubbed in due course by William Shakespeare as belonging to those; "Gentlemen in England now abed, who shall think themselves accursed they were not here, and hold their manhood cheap whilst any speaks that fought with us upon Saint Crispin's day". However, as Thomas was in his sixties at this time, perhaps we should not hold this against him. Moreover the family was already represented in the ranks of Henry's gallant army by William de Northwood who fought both at Harfleur and Agincourt with Henry and was knighted by Henry for his bravery. He was Thomas's cousin and his domain was at Bredhurst near Gillingham.

The earliest referance to a Thanet Norwood is Richard de Northwoode of Ringlow Hundred who is recorded in a subsidy roll of 1327. But there are 6 Norwood wills dating from the last decade of the 15th century, showing the family to be well established in the area of St Peters at Broadstairs. Of these, the most interesting from the perspective of the story of the Dane Court line, from which John Norwood V.C. descends, is Richard, who died in 1485 and his wife Alice; their fourth son Richard was the purchaser of Dane Court and the founder of the line. At the same time, his nephew William Norwood bought Nash court between Margate and Broadstairs. Other Norwoods lived at Callis Court and Duncton Court. The major Kent branches of the Norwood family descend from these acquisitions. Little is known of Richard beyond references in his parents wills. He was probably the deputy from St Peters who attended the General Brotherhood of the Cinque Ports in Romney in July 1525. He died in 1528 and his son Alexander inherited Dane Court. Incidentally, the title had nothing to do with "Danes" but is linked to the word "dell", a small valley.

Richard heads the pedigree in the 1619 Heraldic Visitation which shows a direct descent through Alexander (who died in 1558) to his son, also Alexander (who died in 1583) and to Manasses who died in 1637. Manasses son Richard took over Dane Court and after his death in 1645, his youngest son Paul sold the estate. Dane Court was not however a family home passed from one generation to another but part of their estates. During the lifetime of Manasses, the Norwood fortunes reached their peak with wide interests spread throughout the county, Chilston Park in Boughton Malherbe became the home of Richard with a tenant living in Dane Court.

The Norwoods were no strangers to controversy. After 1534 when the Act of Supremacy asserted Henry VIII to be the Head of the Church of England, it was dangerous to stray away from the new orthodoxy as the priest at St Peters, William Cobbe found to his cost when during Lent he asserted from the pulpit that the Pope had not lost an inch of his authority as a result of recent events. Richard's son Alexander Norwood wrote his treasonous words down, and also drew in another witness, Silvester Terrett, who was standing beside him, to bear witness. Alexander testified as to what he had heard during the Kings visitation to Herne Parish Church on September 18 1536 and the unfortunate priest was then consigned to the King's goal in Canterbury to await the royal pleasure. One assumes that this was a life shortening event unless the priest came up with a convincing recantation.

The dissolution of St Augustine's Abbey in Canterbury which followed soon after in 1539 played another part in the family's advancement. Perhaps owing to Alexander's zeal in the Cobbe affair, he was appointed bailiff and collector of Minster manor which had previously been the property of St Augustine's but which now reverted to the King. Alexander 1 and his wife Joan had at least nine children and they advanced themselves further by some very shrewd marriages. Two children married into the Pettit family, substantial Thanet gentry whose ancestry went back to William FitzMarshall, Earl of Pembroke (died 1231). Adjoining Garlinge is the medieval gate house at Dent-de-Lyon which is all that remains of the Pettit family seat.

Whilst the Norwoods were not recusants (i.e. Anglo Catholics prepared to pay fines rather than attend the new Anglican Church), they were often delinquent in going to mass and therefore subject to a fine of a shilling following the accession of Elizabeth to the throne in 1558. They were also reluctant to pay the local tax for church maintenance. They were however eloquent in their own defence, citing illness and other grounds of indisposition, etc. whilst being ready to pay out to lawyers to defend themselves. The will of Alexander II who died in 1583 demonstrates ample wealth in and land and property so they could afford to do so.

It is clear from a deed of Alexander 1 dated 1540 that he

considered himself to be a yeoman at the very least, that is the class concerned with the land and agriculture. Society in Elizabethan England was intensely hierarchical but the division between yeoman and gentry was not great and the Norwoods of Dane court are to be considered as amongst the minority who made a successful transition. Already in 1558 Alexander elevated his status to the gentry in his will and the same claim was made by his son in 1583. The key test at this time was the right to bear arms, to describe oneself as "armiger" which Manassas Norwood proudly asserts on his tomb.

The period from Manasses' succession to Dane court in 1583 to the outbreak of the Civil War was marked by the rise of his branch of the Norwoods to the peak of their fortunes; they continued to add to their estates and made notable marriages with Thanet and Kent families. A rapid decline then set in; by the early years of the Cromwellian Protectorate, Dane Court was numbered amongst many estates that had been sold, and with the decrease in Norwood lands went a consequential reduction in the family's significance. Manasses obtained the manor of Dene but more importantly he purchased around 1631 from Sir William Tufton the manor of Milton Chasteners, the old Norwood baronial manor with many acres of land. Tufton himself had acquired it from Sir Thomas Norton whose grandmother had been a Norwood heiress. Manasses then consolidated his position by marrying two of his children, Richard and Sarah into the Cleybrookes, a double alliance with local gentry. A third child, Mary married William Duling, son of the Mayor of Rochester; she followed up this marriage upon her widowhood by a marrying Thomas Stanley of West Peckham, another wealthy man.

Manassas sought prominence by furnishing breastplates and

muskets to the local militia, more than any other landowner and added his presence plus that of his sons in law to the muster, earning himself the rank of Captain; the helmet that was at St Peters relates to this time. By now he was a leader of local society. Sometime before his death in 1637 Manassas ceased to reside at Dane Court but nevertheless wished to be buried at St Peters. He was buried in the Chancel and his son Richard obtained permission from the vicar and church wardens to remove some pews in order to inter Manassas and then to make good the damage. This act of filial piety produced the slab of granite that we see today with its many shields, claiming connections in four instances to marriage alliances made with the noble Milton branch of the Norwoods.

Manassas was conscious of his Christian duties and left bequests at St Peters for clothing the poor. His tomb includes a carved

profile. The inscription reads; "Here is laid Manassas Norwood, soldier, of Dane Court who at the age of 70 fell piously asleep in Christ on the 12th day of March in the year of man's salvation 1636". This memorial slab was once on the top of a low altar tomb in the north chancel of the church above which hung Manassas 16th century helmet. Alas the helmet was stolen and the Victorians moved the slab to its present location.

Dane Court in later years.....

The Norwoods showed little reluctance to throw their weight about. There is a document at St Peters which suggests that Richard Norwood was in dispute with the parishioners over the use of the North Chancel which he claimed for the exclusive use of his family. The document is probably dated after 1637 when Manassas died and relates to the period between 1637 and 1642, the outbreak of the civil war. Richard was a Royalist Captain so this is unlikely to have been an issue worthy of pursuit during the conflict and certainly not after the execution of Charles I. The parish was not too pleased about this claim, pointing out that lots of families had relatives buried in the north chancel and that many had contributed to its construction. Although Richard had kicked out his own sometime tenant, Mr. Proud who was working Dane Court at the time, from the chancel into the main body of the church without a fuss, the parishioners pointed out that Richard was not a member of the parish nor did he have family there. There was no ordinance in being that gave exclusive use of any part of the church to anyone!

If Richard had moved from St Peters at this time, it is probably because he had passed the ownership of Dane Court to his son Paul who remained in control until he finally sold it in around 1661 to Richard Smith. Interestingly, maybe the reason why Mr. Proud took his ejection from the chancel without angst is that Paul Norwood was married to Jane Proud, who was presumably his daughter or sister! It is perhaps a reflection of relative status that he was not disposed to rock the family boat.

Richard does seem to have been something of a chancer. There is correspondence between him and his brother in law Thomas Stanley which appears to show that he stinted his mother over her allowance and that this in turn had impacted on her ability to be generous to the Stanleys – Thomas himself emerges as a grasping individual also. National affairs soon impinged on family matters - in 1642 the King raised his standard at Nottingham, and the breach between Crown and parliament broke into open warfare. Throughout the first civil war of 1642-46 there was no fighting in Kent between the armies; Kent remained under Parliamentary control. In the second war of 1648 there was a Royalist rebellion in Kent and disturbances. It is clear that Richards sympathies were Royalist and that he suffered some loss of land as a consequence for being delinquent in not contributing to the Roundhead cause. Stanley was more active and might be termed a moderate Royalist who was engaged in various activities of resistance to Puritan practices and agitation against parliament; he was fined and lost office and land.

In 1640 Richard's daughter Mary married Sir Anthony St Leger of Ulcombe, another useful alliance with a family heavy with knights and sheriffs. He commanded a Regiment of Foot in the King's cause but surrendered in Truro in 1646 and was forced to pay stiff fines and swear allegiance to Parliament. Richard's youngest sister Sarah had married George Somner as a widow in 1640 after the death of William Cleybrooke but he was killed in the Kings cause in 1648. Richard's son Alexander appears to have been locked up in Leeds castle for a while but eventually paid fines and made promises of good behaviour.

Richard died in 1644 and his lands were divided between his three sons, thus beginning the dispersal of property that his father had accumulated. Dane Court and the windmill at St Peters went to his youngest son, Paul. Alexander, the eldest son, inherited substantial properties including Chilston and much land, as well as the manor of Dene but he mismanaged his affairs and was in debt when he died. His widow was at Nash Court when she died in 1706. The property was then sold to a yeoman, David Turner but by a century later, there was little to show for the house which was noted as having little left worthy of notice. The earlier 11th century house was left to rack and ruin after the new Georgian house was built and in the 1940s all that was left was the kitchens and a walled kitchen garden.

Sarah Norwood had a child also called Sarah, by George Somner; she reconnected with the Pettits, who were fervent Royalists, by marrying Captain John Pettit in 1683.   She was the last representative of that period when the Dane Court Norwoods reached the peak of their ascendancy.

Whether Paul Norwood lived in Dane Court after inheriting it, has not been established but it seems unlikely. He sold the property to a Richard Smith in about 1653 ending a connection that had endured for a century and a half. The historian John Harris wrote of Thanet in 1719,"There is not one gentleman who lives in this island, although formerly it was the residence of several ancient and eminent families. But these families are now gone from hence, the estates sold off from the mansion seats and houses converted into farm houses." Dane Court no longer exists and its location is now covered by modern housing at Dane Court Gardens, just behind the St Peters. It was demolished in 1959 after being left vacant during the war years

The Thanet Norwoods were not extinguished by the 17th century but their decline was one of status. Alexander who inherited the bulk of the estates had no sons; the more significant marriages were made by Manassas' daughters and granddaughters and the name Norwood was therefore lost. Moreover, most of the families concerned (the Stanleys are an exception) themselves declined. The key factor was however the dispersal of their lands, the foundation of the social status of a gentleman rested upon his estates; but the sale of lands was a symptom rather than a cause of decline.

.

Chapter 3

The Norwoods of East Peckham

Paul's grandson Richard Norwood (1687- 1773) acquired the small manor of Stilstead just two miles below Roydon Hall on the banks of the Medway, which was at first rented and then purchased from the Twysdens of Roydon, a powerful local family. This transaction was almost in the family as Thomas Stanley, the master of Roydon at the time who had married into the Twysdens was a great grandson of Manassas Norwood. It is this Stilstead line from which John Norwood V.C. is descended.

Records held in the Kent Archives reveal a welter of financial transactions around Stilstead involving numerous mortgages and investing parties. It appears that John Norwood took over the tenancy from Richard in 1771 and bought out the lease in 1788 with other partners. He also owned briefly a farm called Pickfish which adjoined Stilstead in places. It is not quite clear why John's brother Richard, who was the eldest of the two failed to take on Stilstead on John senior's death in 1813. There was however generous provision for him and his siblings, Thomas and Sarah in his father's will. He and his wife Elizabeth received £1600, which depending on the index used, could equate to several million pounds in today's values and presumably compensated him for not taking over Stilstead. An early tithe map of 1823 shows John in residence at Stilstead.

According to "A Kentish Descent" by John Cheesman Norwood, Richard's grandson John (1780-1841), was the third and last generation to possess Stilstead. John Norwood was a typical yeoman farmer, renting other land besides Stilstead; he farmed in all about 600 acres consisting of corn, hops fruit, sheep and cattle. Yet he and his wife rose at 5 a.m. and breakfasted at 7 a.m. with their men and maid servants. His farming was all-round husbandry of corn, hops, fruit, sheep and cattle. His flocks passed to and from Romney Marsh and he raised heavy horned beasts on the lush pastures of the Medway. In about 1824 he sent up to the Smithfield show a bullock 2,920 pounds in weight, said to be the heaviest of the year. He pressed his own cider, brewed his own beer and was one of the last in the district to make cheese. For entertainment, he kept greyhounds and fighting cocks and liked to watch cricket from a wagon serving as a modern stand over the village cricket pitch.

John worked hard and was a prodigious horseman, making on one occasion a round trip of over 90 miles in 24 hours, breakfasting at the Nag's Head in the Borough in Southwark, doing business at Barnet Fair, and returning again to the Nag's Head to lodge for the night. Here however, he found a neighbour having upon him a sum of money which was urgently needed at home on the Weald. Robbery was prevalent, and so at the neighbour's request, he saddled his horse and accompanied him to his destination, reaching his home again within 24 hours.

John and his two brothers were the tallest men in their Yeomanry troop and he was a man of stubborn character. When his father (also John, 1744 -1813) criticised him for the ride, saying angrily that he ought to be ashamed to mount his horse again, his tacit reply was to ride her to another of his farms in Sussex and back again the next day, a distance of 30 miles. The late 1820s were hard times for farmers however and whilst the main farm was still solvent, he sold Stilstead and became manager of a farm owned by his sister in law. His motive may have been to provide a marriage portion for his daughter Sarah but equally could have resulted from an accumulation of debt. Upon his sister in law's death, he turned  to Inn keeping and took on the tenancy of "The Man of Kent" which is very close to Stilstead Farm, where he died in 1841. The large Victorian farm house still on the Stilstead site was built in 1839 and the census for 1851 shows a workforce of 46 men. The original farmhouse was to the right of the driveway to the present buildings and disappeared in the mid-19th century.

Richard is described on his death certificate as a farmer when he also passed away in March 1841 in Tonbridge; his death was witnessed by his brother-in-law Henry Cheesman. His son Richard appears to have forsaken the land because he described himself as a draper when he married Sarah Elizabeth Booker from a High Street address in Dartford in November 1837, but this must have been a passing phase as in the 1841 census when staying with his mother Elizabeth and other siblings in Swan Lane Tonbridge, he identified himself as an engineer. Richard was employed as an official at the railway station in Headcorn in an unclear capacity in July 1843, when son John was born. The station was opened in August 1842 as part of the extension of the South Eastern Railway's mainline from Tonbridge. The line was continued to Ashford by December 1842, to Folkestone by December 1843 and finally to Dover by February 1844. A bridge between Headcorn and Staplehurst was the scene of an accident in 1865 involving Charles Dickens; a rail had been removed by a ganger mistaken as to the train schedule, the flagmen were said to be too close to the potential derailment and the Staplehurst rail crash resulted as carriages flew into a river bed killing ten passengers. Dickens was said to have been permanently effected by his narrow escape which dogged his final years.

Richard's connection with the railway endured because in 1851 we find him in Newark on Trent where he is described as a Railway Inspector of Works. It seems possible that Richard died in Stepney in 1853 shortly after the birth of John his third child. There appears to be no evidence to support the story that he was involved with the Twysdens of Roydon Hall in the building of parts of the South East railway, indeed at this stage of the Norwood's history, their fortunes appeared to be waning. However a railway connection endures because his daughter Kezia married Henry Brown in 1868 at Swanley; Henry was a railway contractor.

Richard's son, John Norwood reconnected the family with their roots by entering the hops trade as a salesman, his profession when he married Lucy Elizabeth Ann Brown in June 1871 in Marylebone. Her father was a builder and Richard is once again described as a draper, although he had died many years since and not in that profession, his widow having remarried a maltster called William Squib at Shoreham in Kent in June 1863. The circumstances of Richard's death and his absences from the family hearth represent something of a mystery. In the 1851 census we find Sarah, described as married, and the children John and Ellen living with her father John Booker who was the proprietor of the Chequers Inn at Eynsford. In the 1861 census she is again with her father at the Chequers but this time only with Ellen. However, now she is described as a widow. By 1881 she has outlived the maltster William (Shoreham, their place of marriage, is just down the valley from Eynsford) and is now found in Edmonton, London, a 65 year old woman of independent means whose daughter Ellen, now a certificated teacher, is with her aged 35. We shall hear more of Ellen later when she travels to South Africa to marry Alfred Adams, a missionary with the London Missionary Society and a disciple of Livingstone.

The hops business underwent something of a boom from the mid-19th century stimulated by increased population and the growth in industrialised towns propelling a demand for beer, which is well documented by Margaret Lawrence the Kent historian. As a result, the English hop acreage doubled between 1800 and 1870. In East Peckham, the Hop Tithe records show that 53 people were growing hops on land ranging from a half to 49 acres. If John Norwood had been able to hang on a little longer, or the boom had started earlier, he would have been a wealthy man. In 1862 the affluence of both brewers and growers grew when profits increased through the removal of the Hop excise duty. Such was the expansion however that labour was sucked in from the poor and unemployed of the East End of London leading to social dislocation and disturbances; it was not until about 1879 after a campaign by philanthropists to provide humane conditions that farmers were required to provide basic accommodation and facilities for hop pickers which brought order and sobriety.

John was able to ride this boom successfully. The couple's

first born Amy arrived in March 1872 which found the couple at 2 Manor Road Deptford. This road is now an Avenue and no 4 is a considerable four story property. By 1878 and the birth of John Norwood, the family had moved to Beckenham, a burgeoning village on the outskirts of London poised between the hops country and the hops market centred on the Borough High Street.

The hop trade was a significant part of Southwark's commercial past until the early 1970s. Southwark was for centuries associated with hops, breweries and coaching inns. The inns derived their existence from the fact that Borough High Street and Old London Bridge constituted the only land route into the City from the south until as late as 1750. All the road traffic from Kent, Surrey and Sussex came through Southwark. Southwark's hops came from Kent. The symbol of their origin may be seen in the local Hop Exchange: Kent's county arms of a white horse on a red background, is repeated endlessly on the galleries of the Exchange's hall. When the hops had been picked in the autumn, they were traditionally taken to oast-houses for drying, and then packed into what the world might call sacks, but which were known in the trade as "pockets", these were taken to Southwark and stored in the hop warehouses. All this was done under the aegis of middlemen known as hop factors, who acted on behalf of the growers. They made their living by charging the growers commission. In Southwark, the "pockets" were sampled, that is to say, a piece weighing about one pound was carefully cut out to be examined more closely. The hop factors had showrooms in Southwark, where the samples were once inspected by buyers in these showrooms who were the hop merchants, another set of middlemen who acted on behalf of the brewers

Wigans were the biggest firm of hop merchants and had several warehouses. In 1864, in the newly-laid out Southwark Street, the firm commissioned R.P. Pope, an architect who had a thriving local commercial practice, to build a warehouse at No. 61 capable of holding 10,000 pockets and having a facility to load and unload four wagons at one time under cover. But even more storage was needed. So in 1868, when a body called the Hop Planters' Joint Stock Company went into liquidation, its property at No.15 Southwark Street was bought by Wigans, and was massively extended towards the Charing Cross railway viaduct. This immense warehouse empire came in an era when Excise figures show that the annual hops crop regularly reached between 500,000 and 600,000 hundred weights and as much as 797,000 in 1855. The firm ran a cricket team, of which it was inordinately proud, and one advertisement for staff in 1903 included the line, 'only cricketers need apply'. The firm's head for some decades was Sir Frederick Wigan, one of Victorian Southwark's merchant princes. This was the environment in which John Norwood built a successful career.

The Norwood home, then called Pembury Lodge, still stands at Number 65 Copers Cope road, a leafy avenue built in the 1870's to accommodate the large families, servants and carriages of the prosperous middle class. In the 1881 census John is described as a hops merchant, which suggests that he was doing well, a judgement supported by the cook, parlour maid and housemaid also listed at the house. He had no coach man, at least in residence, but perhaps this was unnecessary as New Beckenham station is about 50 yards away offering a short and convenient hop to the city.

The young John was sent to the Abbey School, an establishment for young gentlemen founded in 1866 by the Reverend Lloyd

Philips assisted by his sister Elizabeth and located at Brackley Road, a very short walk away. It was typical of the schools set up to cater for the new wealthy and was described in 1892 as the biggest and best private school in Kent. Boys had private dormitory cubicles, and even a carpentry shop. There was a separate Sanatorium with an isolation unit, for even in the best areas typhoid, diphtheria and cholera were not yet stamped out. Photographs that survive of the lavishly appointed dining room show pictures and sporting trophies of the kind that might grace an Oxford dining hall. It was evidently a good preparation for the school life to come at Rugby.

The parish church of St Pauls was conveniently close at hand having been built in 1872 to serve the community. It contains a reference to John Norwood on its memorial plaque to the dead of the 1914-18 War albeit ascribing to him the wrong rank of Lieutenant Colonel (another plaque has been raised to him and his relative, Second Lieutenant John Norton Norwood of the 4th Royal Inniskilling Fusiliers in the old parish church of St Michael at East Peckham). The family's next door neighbour at no 63, J.C. Hewlett was a church warden at St Pauls.

John must have had quite a testing childhood; his mother died in 1890 at Bromley when he was 12 and on the verge of going away to Rugby. His father died on 14 September 1896 at Liverpool where he was on business. Both are buried in a rather imposing well preserved grave in West Norwood cemetery, in that part of the cemetery that has been allowed to revert to nature. He was evidently a senior figure at Wigans and Crosier as witnesses to the will were Robert Watson

Crosier of 15 Southwark Street and John Gretton Wigan of 8A Lord Street Liverpool, hops agent whom he was probably visiting at the time of his death. His executors were his brother in law Henry Brown and Stuart Neame of 33 Borough High Street; Neame was a member of the well-known Kent family which still has major brewing interests. John senior left his children well provided for; the bulk of his legacy was left to them and was probated at around £34,000, a significant sum in those days. He left some money to his sister Kezia Brown, the wife of Henry and also to another sister, Ellen Adams of Eshowe, Natal. The lives of the Brown and Adams family were closely entwined, as the personal history John Norwood V. C. later reveals.

It is clear that John Norwood had to take Maths, Latin and Greek to get into Oxford and went on to study Religion, fairly commonplace choices. However he also took courses in law which may indicate one possible direction of his thinking. He passed the first part of the First Public Examination for his degree and the preliminary part of the Second Public Examination but he did not go on to complete his degree. He left Oxford after the Hilary term in 1998, which commences in January. As we know that he founded a Masonic Lodge at Exeter College, loved country pursuits such as shooting and riding and became involved with the Army whilst still at University, we must assume that he lead a busy life. It was probably not unusual in the gilded days of the late 1890s for wealthy students to go up to Oxford to enjoy College life without being overly concerned about a degree. He had other ideas about his future- he joined the Army.

John moved after his father's death to a smaller property along Coper's Cope Road at number 56A which was called

"Voewood"; where he lived in 1898 and 99. By some extraordinary coincidence, John's surname was subsequently misspelled as "Vowood" on the War Memorial at Sablonnieres where he was killed. In 1899 John was gazetted as a Second Lieutenant and from surviving photographs appears to have been a tall rather imposing young man. He was quickly posted to India with the 5th (Princess Charlotte of Wales) Dragoon Guards and at the outbreak of the Boer War looked for action.

Chapter 4

The Fifth Dragoon Guards

John Norwood came from a relatively affluent background, but it is doubtful that he could have afforded to join the 5th Dragoons before the major change that took place in November 1871 with the abolition of the purchase of commissions. Previously, all officers belonged to or were dependant on a class who were prepared to pay a considerable sum to find a career for their sons without any prospect of ceasing to support them. The sequel to this change was the bestowal of commissions on successful candidates in a competitive examination, which is how John succeeded. Some of the senior officers under whom John served in the Boer War would however have come from the old system. The Cardwell changes of 1872 also introduced enlistment of the men for 12 years rather than for life, although NCOs were expected to serve longer. Another change that affected the 5th Dragoons from 1889 was the abolition of Heavy Cavalry, previously requiring bigger horses and taller heavier men. The development of modern weaponry made the distinctions between Heavy, Light and Medium regiments impossible to sustain. Regiments were brigaded henceforth without regard to their prior classification. There remained a tendency to try and recruit bigger men on the sensible grounds that they were likely to be healthier and offer fewer disciplinary problems (this was said to be based on experience) although the standard of behaviour in the Heavy Cavalry was traditionally good.

It is clear from the Regimental record that the 5th Dragoons were quite fashionable, frequently providing escorts and guards to Queen Victoria and members of the Royal family, changing places at times with the Household Cavalry and undertaking guard duties at Windsor. The regiment also served frequently in Ireland, in Dublin and at the Curragh apart from Aldershot, Canterbury and other places in support of the civil power.

The Regiment received its first breech loading weapon in 1868 which was slung behind the riders leg and by 1892, it was armed with the Martini Metford carbine which in one form or another, took it through to the outbreak of war in 1914. In 1890 it was decided to arm the front ranks of the Regiment with the lance in a defiant riposte to a school of thought in the infantry that the cavalry would be of little service in future wars. Perversely, the cavalry believed that a weapon that they had used as an adjunct to training since 1817 had a part to play in open warfare and this was indeed demonstrated in the Boer war during the charge at Elandslagte in which John Norwood took part against a mounted enemy. It was however discontinued after the Boer War apart from regiments stationed in India.

The introduction of khaki was to revolutionize the dress of the British Army from about 1885 onwards but the Dragoons stood out for a period for their somewhat colourful attire. In 1882 a detachment of Dragoons sent to Egypt wore red serge, jacked boots and pouch belts and sabretaches – a somewhat ornate flat bag, which was worn suspended from the belt of a cavalry officer together with the sabre. We should not forget also the brass helmet which had peaks fore and aft, a chain chin strap and a socket and plume on top. A painting of charging troopers made in 1908 indicates nostalgia for past glories.

A great deal of time was naturally spent on training in order to ensure that the Regiment was able to complete all the necessary battlefield manoeuvres expected of the cavalry without losing shape and position. In 1876 there was an introduction in a new drill book of movement "by fours" through which 8 men abreast, four front and four rear ranks, were trained to wheel as a unit. Every detail of training was specified, down to the trot speed of 8 miles an hour to the gallop at 12 miles an hour and the charge was defined as "not to exceed the speed of the slowest horse". Horsemanship was the key to effectiveness but unlike the principles behind cavalry elsewhere in the world, by this time, a new principle was established which succinctly stated "Now that Cavalry are armed with the breech loading rifled carbine, dismounted service is of great importance and must be constantly practiced".

Probably the best expression of the Cavalry role in the world that John occupied until his death in 1914 is contained in a preface to a book on training written by Lord Roberts in 1904. "Cavalry must now be considered not only as the eyes of an army and the arm by which a demoralised enemy can best be destroyed, but equipped with the new short rifle, it will take a part in war which it has never been able to take in the past.....the change that has taken place in Cavalry is as great as that which occurred to the Infantry when the crossbow and pike were replaced by the rifle and bayonet. When Cavalry was first organised, Lancer Regiments depended entirely on the lance and sword owing to the short range, inaccuracy and difficulty in loading the smooth bore musket and carbine. With such equipment and traditions, it was perhaps natural that the training of Cavalry should have been almost exclusively devoted to shock tactics and the use of *d'arme blanche,* (any cutting or bladed weapon, usually a sword or lance) in spite of the recognised fact that for many years past, it has not been possible for Cavalry to act effectively against unbroken Infantry."

"But what does the development of rifle fire, consequent on the introduction of the long range, low trajectory, magazine rifle mean? It means that instead of the firearm being an adjunct to the sword, the sword must henceforth be an adjunct to the rifle and that cavalry soldiers must become expert rifle shots and be constantly trained to act dismounted."

"Training Cavalry Officers need have no fear that training their men to fight on foot as well as on horseback will in anyway interfere with the *elan* which is so essential for cavalry soldiers to possess. I trust that Cavalry officers will not allow themselves to entertain the idea that I do not see the utility of shock tactics.

This is far from being the case. The Cavalry spirit is one to be maintained at all costs in our mounted services."

If John Norwood had not been a first class horseman on entering the 5th Dragoons, he was certainly expected to be so not long after.

The Regiment had one conspicuous action to its credit before its long sojourn in India where John Norwood joined it after leaving University. This may have inspired his choice of regiment. This was the action at Abu Klea, the first steps of the gallant but failed attempt to save General Gordon in Khartoum from his self-inflicted fate at the hands of the Mahdi, a Moslem fanatic whose religious fervour had gripped the minds of his Sudanese followers. This was the kind of action that stirred the blood of Victorian schoolboys and swelled the ranks of both officers and men.

Gordon, an eccentric British Royal Engineer Officer, had served the Khedive (the Ruler of Egypt, owing nominal fealty to the Ottoman Emperor) as Governor of Equatoria and as Governor General of the Sudan. He was a deeply religious man who felt that his destiny was to suppress the Sudanese slave trade. After the Mahdist successes against the forces of the Egyptian Government from 1881 onwards, it was clear that all British and Egyptian citizens in the Sudan were at risk so Gordon's instruction was to report back on the prospect of evacuation. He arrived in early February 1884 without incident. But in that month an Egyptian force commanded by Lieutenant General Baker Pasha was eliminated by Dervishes in the eastern Sudan at El Teb. The British sent a British force to El Teb who then defeated the Dervishes but there was no appetite for further engagement and the Mahdists began a siege of Khartoum in March. Very reluctantly and in face of public opinion, the

Government put together a force to save Gordon. Their reluctance derived from the conviction that he had forced the Government to intervene in the Sudan when their preferred course was evacuation.

A key decision was route selection; General Wolsey, who was in charge of the rescue, preferred the 1426 mile route up the Nile, but other officers argued for the 245 miles route from Suakin on the Red Sea to Berber. By September 1884 the Nile expedition was ready to start but in parallel a decision was made to send another force to set out west from the Red Sea port of Suakin with the goal of laying a narrow gauge railway to the Nile and

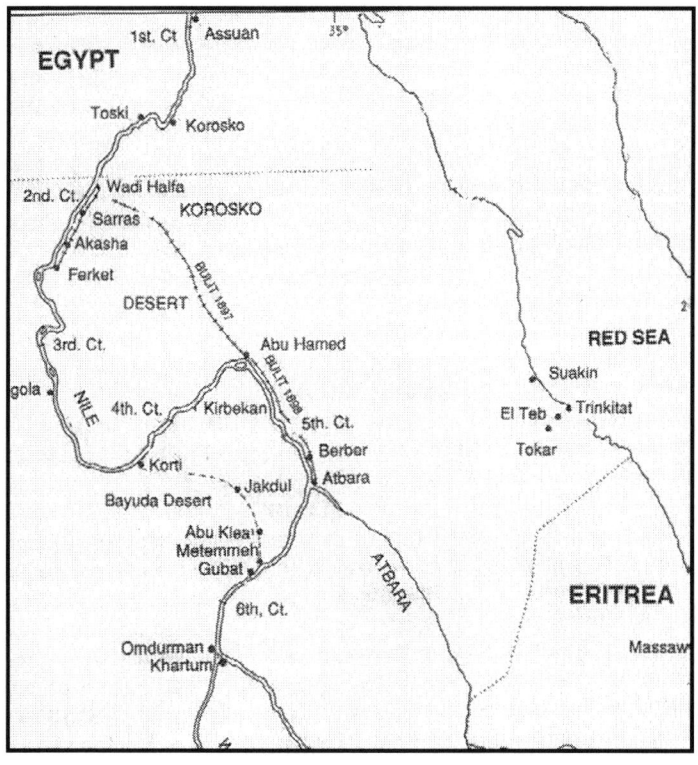

winning the race to relieve Khartoum. It ended up being embroiled with tribesmen from the Beja tribe known to history as the "Fuzzies Wuzzies" (allies of the Mahdi) because of the way that they used cow fat to grease their hair and turn it into an effective helmet as a defence against the sun. The railway project was too ambitious and the attacks relentless.

The Beja provided a large number of warriors (or Dervishes) to the Mahdist forces. They were armed with swords and spears and some of them carried breech-loaded rifles which had been captured from the Egyptian forces. Others had acquired military experience in the Egyptian army. In Kipling's poem "Fuzzy-Wuzzy", his fictional narrator, an infantry soldier praises

the Hadendowa (Beja) for their martial prowess, because "for all the odds agin' you, Fuzzy-Wuz, you broke the square", which, although insufficient to defeat the British, did at least enable them to boast of an achievement which few other British foes could claim. This poem could refer to either or both historical battles between the British Army and Mahdist forces where British infantry squares, the preferred battle formation of the time, were broken. The first was at the Battle of Tamai, on 13 March 1884, and the second was at Abu Klea.

In the Suakin expedition, serving as a senior officer, was John Norwood's future father in law, Edwin Collen who eventually rose to General, and indeed became the most senior man in the Indian Army as Military Secretary to the Viceroy of India, before bring knighted for his services. In the future, as Military Secretary he was destined to fight a losing battle with Kitchener over control of Army reform in attempting to support Lord Curzon's attempt to maintain the supremacy of the Viceroy's Council and thereby Curzon's own power. The painting of him in his early twenties by his father, the renowned miniaturist Henry Collen shows him wearing the Abyssinian Medal following his participation in the campaign to overthrow the Emperor Theodorus in 1868.

The Graham expedition had withdrawn after crushing the Dervishes at the second action at El Teb on 29 February and relieving the town of Tokar, so they knew what faced them on their return. The dervishes were led by a charismatic figure called Osman Digna. Despite his earlier victory Graham realised that Digna's force was far from broken and that he still enjoyed support among the local population. Accordingly, a second expedition departed from Suakin on 10 March in order to defeat the Mahdists definitively.

The force was composed of the same units that had fought at El Teb: 4,500 men, with 22 guns and 6 machine guns. The Mahdists had roughly 10,000 men, most of them belonging to Osman's tribe. On the night of 12 March the British formed an encampment, not far from Osman Digna's positions. From around 1 o'clock until dawn, Mahdist riflemen approached the camp and opened fire, but their shooting was imprecise, and they inflicted few casualties.

At dawn, the artillery was brought to bear against the Mahdist skirmishers and they were driven back. The infantry (which included the Black Watch) then formed into two infantry squares each of brigade-size and advanced. One square was commanded by Colonel Davis, with General Graham, and the other by Colonel Buller. A scouting party discovered that the main body of the Mahdist force was hidden in a nearby ravine, whereupon General Graham ordered the Black Watch to charge to clear those Mahdists out, leaving a wide gap where they had been stationed in the square. A sudden onslaught of Mahdists rushed into this gap. The Black Watch found themselves under intense attack from the Sudanese. The square was flooded with a rush of tribesmen and a brutal hand-to-hand fight resulted. The Black Watch eventually won the contest, driving the Sudanese out, and reforming their square.

Finding themselves in danger of being cut off, the British units fell back in disarray but were quickly reformed in good order. The Mahdist advance was halted by volleys from the other (Buller's) square, which had survived the attack, and by dismounted cavalry units that had not been engaged until then. The concentrated flanking fire they inflicted caused huge casualties among the Mahdists, who were forced to retreat. The British units then reformed, and resumed their advance, driving the shaken Mahdists out of the ravine and inflicting more casualties on them as they fled. Digna's camp was captured later that day, but he escaped. He was later seized however and imprisoned in Egypt.

During this battle, the British suffered more losses than in any other battle of the Mahdist war, 214 soldiers being wounded or killed, ten of which were officers. The Mahdists also suffered heavily, losing 4,000 men. The site of this battle is marked today by an obelisk which still stands tall and straight in its lonely place in the desert, far from any road, about two metres high. Its four sides once contained slabs listing the names of the fallen but they have dropped away over the 130 years or so since this battle. The nearby ravine (or wadi) in which the dervishes hid is plainly visible and it is clear that the local Beja people are very proud of their part in history when Kipling celebrated their breaking of the square and their near-defeat of the British Army.

John Norwood's future father in law was at General Graham's right hand during this engagement. He then held the rank of Major and ran the Intelligence Department but he participated in the actions at Tamai and Thakool, was mentioned in despatches and received the Bronze Medal and clasp, the Bronze Star and the Brevet of Lieutenant Colonel for his pains. In his despatch, Graham wrote "Major EHH Collen is an officer of exceptional ability and experience. He is an excellent staff officer and has given me most valuable assistance as Military Secretary."

In September 1884 the 5th Dragoons were called upon to provide 2 Officers, a handful of NCOs and 38 soldiers to join the Heavy Division of the Camel Corps sent to Egypt as part of the river expedition to relieve Gordon. The force was drawn from a miscellany of Cavalry Regiments; the men had to be marksmen or first class shots, over 22, medically fit and of good character. They were armed with rifle and sword bayonet and wore a bandolier holding 50 cartridges. Significantly, their dress was khaki and they wore puttees, ankle boots and a pith sun helmet. They arrived in Alexandria in October and by January were assembled on the Nile at Gardul with elements of the Naval Brigade, the Middlesex and Sussex Regiments and the Marines ready to march across the desert to Metammeh where they were to join another column for the final march on Khartoum, a further 100 miles up the river. They exchanged their horses for camels and the total strength of the force consisted of about 1600 men, 2300 camels and 90 horses. There was a degree of urgency around the rescue effort at this stage as Gordon was now under great pressure in Khartoum having lost any chance of evacuation.

On the fourth day of marching, the wells of Abu Klea came in sight but the tribesmen were out in force and ready to fight. On January 17 1885 the force advanced in the shape of the classic square and soon came under heavy fire. The 5th were in the rear of the advancing square which was suddenly attacked by a force concealed in a nullah from the left front. A bulge developed in the square, throwing the left face into disorder. This was followed by an enormous mass of the enemy bearing down on the left flanks, causing the 5th and 4th Dragoons to about- face to deal with the threat. At this moment, the Naval Brigade's Gardener gun jammed considerably reducing available firepower.

The Gardner gun was an early type of mechanical machine gun. It had up to five barrels, was fed from a vertical magazine or hopper and was operated by a crank. When the crank was turned, a feed arm positioned a cartridge in the breech, the bolt closed and the weapon fired. Turning the crank further opened the breechblock and extracted the spent case. In the furious fighting that followed, Colonel Fred Burnaby a legendary Victorian man of action, was killed out in front of the 5th, the enemy entered the square where they were dealt with by bayonet. Steady fire, killing many of the enemy leaders, finally broke the Arab force, which fled leaving 1100 dead on the field. Total British losses amounted to 74 killed and 94 wounded, of which the 5th's losses were 11 killed and 7 wounded.

The famous war artist Melton Prior, who was to have a future role in John Norwood's life, was present during this battle. He wrote in his diary that on January 17th after a night laying down under continuous rifle fire, General Sir Herbert Stewart formed up the square, losing men as he did so from the hills on either side. Skirmishers had been instructed to scout out ahead but to fall back on the flanks of the square once the enemy was sighted, but the Arabs leapt up from a donga and forgetting their orders, they retreated on the front of the square, thus inhibiting fire from that quarter on the attackers. The Mahdi force then attacked the front corner of the square at the moment that the machine gun jammed, and killed all of the wounded who were hanging in slings from camels. The square could only be cleared by firing across it, injuring friend and foe alike. Burnaby was killed by being speared in the back of the neck trying to save two soldiers. The enemy then wavered and broke after taking volley after volley of fire. The slaughter was great.

During the night, Prior hired an Egyptian camel driver to carry his drawings of the campaign as well as despatches from the war

 correspondent James Cameron of the Standard to a supply post at Gakdul and thence via Korti to Cairo for onward transmission. He was almost certainly murdered en route. The night was so dark that the column became confused and having lost the road, Prior's forces ended up joining the rear of the column without realising it, going in circles for two hours. Only as morning broke was the mistake discovered and order restored. By this time the British were about 4 miles from the Nile. At dawn a zareeba was formed and the men given breakfast, but they did not have long to eat it.

At 0700 hours, Mahdist forces continued their onslaught initially from a distance of 1400 yards, nonetheless exacting a heavy toll of casualties; journalists were not spared as Prior's good friend John Cameron was amongst the dead. Everything was done to induce the Mahdists to close the range but they held off and firing took place over 7 hours. It was eventually decided to form up into a square and head straight for the enemy and the Nile, but such was the intensity of fire that 25 men were killed whilst this was done; the square continued to suffer heavily from sniping during its advance and became so encumbered by more wounded that it looked as if it might not be able to continue. However, not realising the success of their tactics, the Arabs shaped up to attack. The square halted, closed ranks and held its fire until the enemy was within 300 yards. Their devastating firepower mowed down their adversary who broke and fled. Amongst the casualties was General Sir Herbert Stewart, the commander of the expedition, who was shot in the groin and died later. Although Melton Prior was a war artist and not a journalist, his diary gives a vivid account of the action.

"And now our whole attention was directed towards the square. The men marched forward with teeth clenched, grasping their rifles, determined to do or die and uphold the glory, prestige and tradition of British arms; for surely it was a case of victory or death - nay of annihilation itself, but their hearts never faltered for a moment. Their faces never looked blanched, although pulses may have quickened and muscles grow tense as they saw the enemy from a distance of about 500 yards, prepared to swoop down like an avalanche upon the little valorous band."

"Our square consisted of only 800 men all told, and although the flanks were moved out to act with the front face, there could not have been more than 400 engaged in the fight. All were ordered to fire only by command - the front rank kneeling."

"400 men alone, think of it! And a fanatical host of 10,000 to 12,000 with waving banners yells and flashing spears, caring not for death, willing to die, glad to die at the hand of the infidel. Surging down over the sand like a mighty inundation against the solid little square which received the impact like a rock. Three times were they sent reeling back as volley after volley was poured into them. Three times they rallied, but in vain. The desert sand was three deep with their slain. The British square was invincible and as steady as on parade. Then came a sudden stampede. The enemy bolted, panic stricken. Cheers rose from British throats and the square in perfect order pushed on for the Nile and camped there for the night." Prior carried one of the wounded on his back to safety (a strange early reflection of the action which earned John Norwood his V.C.)

A fortified camp was set up on the Nile and on the next day the force continued its advance on Metammeh. The position of the column was however still critical as General Earle's Nile column had not yet arrived. They were unable to seize Metammeh, a village of baked mud huts, which was well defended whilst the attackers were exposed in the open and the attack was abandoned. Several days later, boats were seen on the river.

Prior records; "Looking up the river, (on 22 January) I saw four extraordinary looking things coming down. They were evidently boats, for they had funnels and any amount of black smoke was pouring out. Are they friend or foe, was Gordon on board or had Khartoum fallen? Casting anchor, they swung around. They looked exactly like the London County Council penny steamboats turned into floating forts by means of railway sleepers and sheet iron and contained those who had remained faithful to Gordon Pasha and the British cause. The Commander in Chief was Kashem-el-Moos, a fine looking old Egyptian."

It was clear that Khartoum had fallen but an attempt was nonetheless made to confirm that Gordon was dead involving a lone steamer and pinnace making their way upstream carrying 150 of Gordon's Sudanese soldiers and 20 members of the Sussex Regiment. After a fierce skirmish at Omdurman, the small force withdrew and then the steamer was wrecked, requiring rescue. Gordon was evidently dead; he died on the steps of his residence  on 26 January. The best evidence suggests that Gordon went out to confront the enemy, gunned down several of the Mahdists with his revolver and after running out of bullets, drew his sword only to be shot down. He was then decapitated. For the relief expedition, there was nothing for it but to retreat. In the hours following Gordon's death an estimated 10,000 civilians and members of the garrison were killed in Khartoum.

Gordon's death caused a huge wave of national grief all over Britain with 13 March 1885 being set aside as a day of mourning for the "fallen hero of Khartoum". In a sermon, the Bishop of Chichester stated: "Nations who envied our greatness rejoiced now at our weakness and our inability to protect our trusted servant. "Stones were thrown at the windows at 10 Downing Street as Gladstone was denounced as the "Murderer of Gordon", the Judas figure who betrayed the Christ figure Gordon. The wave of mourning was not just confined to

Britain. In New York, Paris and Berlin, pictures of Gordon appeared in shop windows with black lining as all over the West the fallen general was seen as a Christ-like man who sacrificed himself resisting the advance of Islam.

Despite the popular demand to "avenge Gordon", the Conservative government that came into office after the 1885 election , throwing out Gladstone, did nothing of the sort as the Sudan was judged to be not worth the huge financial costs it would have taken to conquer it, the same conclusion that the Liberals had reached. It would not be until 1898 that the British exacted their revenge again at Omdurman with the re-conquest of the Sudan. In the meantime, the expedition including the 5th Dragoons was back in Alexandria by July and at home not long afterwards.

Prior's sketches were eventually published in his magazine "The Illustrated London News" as the art of war photography was still in its infancy and certainly not available for campaigns like these. Breathless accounts of the action by Bennet Burleigh of the Daily Telegraph, Frederick Villiers of the Graphic and HHS Pearce of the Daily News, amongst others, no doubt excited public opinion and impressed themselves on the minds of school boys like John Norwood who probably imagined themselves on the backs of charging steeds. In the meantime, Prior went on in the coming years to cover a punitive expedition to Burma in 1887, the Jameson raid into South Africa, the Afridi campaign on the Northern Frontier of India in 1897 (in which a small contingent of 5th Dragoons participated), the Cretan rising against the Turks also in '97 and then the Anglo South African war where he reconnected with the 5th Dragoon Guards at the Siege of Ladysmith.

Prior was a remarkable and courageous war correspondent who died in London on 2 November 1910 at his home in Lee Green. His body is buried at Hither Green Cemetery in Lewisham in an unmarked grave under the remains of a fallen tree and he received a glowing obituary even as far afield as the USA in the New York Times. He was married twice but had no heirs.

Chapter 5

The Fifth Dragoons in India

John Norwood joined the 5th in India, to where they were posted from 1893 to 1899 initially to Meerut and then later to Sialkote to join the" Army of India", as opposed to the "Indian Army" which appears to have been first used informally, as a collective description of the Bengal, Madras and the Bombay Armies of the Presidencies of British India, particularly after the Indian Mutiny of 1857. The first army officially called the "Indian Army" was raised by the government of India in 1895, existing alongside the three long-established Presidency armies. However, Lord Kitchener was Commander-in-Chief, India, between 1902 and 1909 and instituted large-scale reforms, the greatest of which was the merger of the three

Armies of the Presidencies into a unified force. As the photo shows, Sialkote was pretty rustic.

Kitchener formed higher level formations, eight army divisions, and brigaded Indian and British units. Following Kitchener's reforms: the Indian Army was the force recruited locally and permanently based in India, together with its expatriate British officers: the British Army in India consisted of British Army units posted to India for a tour of duty, after which they would be posted to other parts of the Empire or back to the UK: the term "Army of India" consisted of both the Indian Army and the British Army in India.

The principles underlying the reforms were that the army's primary role was defence of the North-West Frontier against foreign aggression (for which read "the threat from Russia"); all units were to have training and experience in that role on that frontier; the army's organisation should be the same in peace as in war; maintaining internal security was for the army a secondary role, in support of the police.

Lord Kitchener found the Army scattered across the country in stations at brigade or regimental strength, and in effect, providing garrisons for most of the major cities. In contrast, the reformed Indian Army was to be stationed in operational formations and concentrated in the north of the sub-continent. The Commander-in-Chief's plan called for nine fighting divisions grouped in two corps commands stationed along the main axes through the North-West Frontier. Five divisions were to be grouped on the Lucknow – Peshawar – Khyber axis, and four divisions on the Bombay – Mhow – Quetta axis.

Under the compromise adopted in 1905, the four existing commands were reduced to three, and together with Army Headquarters, were arranged in ten standing divisions and four independent brigades: Northern Command comprised the 1st (Peshawar) Division, the 2nd (Rawalpindi) Division, the 3rd (Lahore) Division, the Kohath Brigade, the Banyu, and the Brigade. Western comprised the 4th (Quetta) Division, the 5th (Mhow) Division, the 6th (Poona) Division, and the Aden Brigade, located in Aden in the Arabian Peninsula; Eastern comprised the 7th (Meerut) Division and the 8th (Lucknow) Division. The 5th were part of this Command. Army Headquarters retained the 9th (Secunderabad) Division and the Burma Division under its direct control The numbered divisions were organised so that on mobilisation they could deploy a complete infantry division, a cavalry brigade, and a number of troops for internal security or local frontier defence. Permanent divisional commands were formed with an establishment of staff officers under a Major-General.

The Indian Army would of course make a major contribution on the Western Front, in Mesopotamia and in Palestine in the First World War but the 19th century is studded with examples of the deployment of forces from India to further British interests in Africa and the Middle East and in South East Asia, not excluding China during the Boxer Rebellion and three wars in Afghanistan. A keen young soldier was more likely to see action in the late 19th century in the Indian Army than anywhere else.

Just before John Norwood's arrival in India, the 5th sent a contingent of troops to take part in the Tyrah Expedition, the largest and most serious outbreak of fighting on the North West Frontier during the colonial era. They had machine guns and all the modern firepower that was thought to be necessary to put down a tribal rising. This Pathan (or Afridi) uprising of 1897-8 was

actually a series of local insurrections involving over 200,000 fighters, including Afghan volunteers, and it required over 59,000 regular troops and 4,000 Imperial Service Troops to deal with it; the largest deployment in India since the Mutiny of 1857-8. Its outbreak proved such an unexpected and significant shock to the British that they conducted detailed enquiries after the event.

Various explanations were offered for the uprising but it is generally accepted that recent encroachments into tribal territory, with fears that the British meant to permanently occupy the region as a prelude to the destruction of Pathan independence and way of life, led to the initial fighting. There were other contributory factors: a perception that the Amir of Afghanistan, Abdur Rahman Khan, would support an anti-British Jihad; rumours that the Christian Greeks had been defeated by the Muslim Turks and that the Christian world was finally in retreat, and local anxieties about women, money-lenders and road-building.

The campaign was bloody, involving attacks by the British on sheer defended heights held by well-armed tribesmen. There were a constant stream of small scale skirmishes and if the British concentrated forces to deal with a suspected strong point, the tribesmen would disperse before the British could track them down. This was guerilla warfare in some of the world's most inhospitable terrain on the North West frontier such as the Swat valley that has become all too familiar since. To make matters worse, the tribesmen had acquired breech-loading rifles on a large scale for the first time on the frontier and so the ranges and effectiveness of the fire was more deadly than anything that the British had experienced before Some of the actions were the stuff of legend- at the battle of Dargai Heights,

HEAD QUARTER CAMP FORT LOCKHART.
Looking towards Tirah.

From a sketch by—
Lieut. E. H. Collen, R. A.,
13th October 1897.

involving three infantry charges across open ground, five Victoria Crosses were awarded for the action, but the casualty list saw 4 officers killed, 34 enlisted men killed, 14 officers and 147 enlisted men wounded. The Afridi treated captured wounded British soldiers no better than the Taliban or Islamic State regard their victims today.   Eventually the Pathans accepted terms and probably regarded the outcome as a draw - there were lessons here for future conflict on the border 100 years hence.

Lieutenant EH Collen of the Royal Artillery took part in the Tyra expedition and drew many sketches of the battle fields and the

terrain in general. He was an accomplished artist. Later of course be became the brother in law of John Norwood for whom he was a near contemporary and with whom he served in South Africa as well as the First World War.

Queen Victoria had her own reservations about the Tyrah campaign; in a letter to the Viceroy she wondered if the raising of Field Forces to subdue the area was the most effective policy 'As we did not wish to retain any part of the country, is the continuation and indefinite prolongation of these punitive expeditions really justifiable at the cost of many valuable lives?".

Outside of the action on the frontier, life in India tended to be rather dull. From April to September, the climate was so intolerable that there was little to do but sleep from two hours after sunrise to two hours before sunset, but the heat made sleep almost impossible except when the rains broke. Sport was essential and the great institution in India was of course polo which was played three times a week – polo ponies were relatively cheap. There was also pig sticking, using a lance on wild pigs and tent pegging, rather more humane. Thursday was a complete day off, unlike Sundays, which whilst notionally a day of rest involved parades and church attendance etc. During the cold weather period from October to March, even with an average of 4 hours in bed, there was a lot to do in terms of training which included manoeuvres and inter Regiment competitions – the 5th won the Commander in Chief's prize for British Cavalry in 1894 and beat 37 teams from infantry regiments to take the individual attack competition in the Bengal Presidency in the same year.

John Norwood as a handsome young subaltern with a strong physique was probably courted by the expatriate community and of course had the unusual advantage of knowing the only daughter of the Military Secretary from their schooldays in England. Lilian Blanche Collen was educated at Beckenham alongside Amy Norwood, John's only sister and met him at the family home when he was still a youngster. Other status issues aside, the acquaintance ensured that he was persona grata at events in Delhi and Shimla when the Administration retreated to the hills for the hot season. Lilian in turn was a handsome young woman with a strong spirit of independence, so they were well matched. He soon took off for a solo hunting adventure which he recorded conscientiously in a diary and which shows him at his impetuous best. Most officers were keen on shooting; they could get duck, snipe and various partridges near most cantonments; tiger, bear, panther, bison buffalo and various kinds of stag in the jungles. But the cream of the sport was the pursuit of the, ibex and markhor as well as ovis ammon, the largest species of wild sheep, found largely in Central Asia, bearing magnificent horns.

Chapter 6

An Expedition to Kashmir

John Norwood organised a hunting trip to Kashmir on August 18 1899 from his base in Sialkote. He took a slow train to Rawalpindi and then hired a Tonga to travel on to Barmulla on the frontier with Kashmir. A Tonga is a light carriage. It has a canopy over the carriage with a single pair of large wheels. The passengers reach the seats from the rear while the driver sits in front of the carriage. Some space is available for baggage below the carriage, between the wheels. This was often used to carry hay for the horses. He passed through the finest scenery that he had ever seen and then hired a boat to take him up Wolla Lake.

He was high handed with the locals pestering him for work, throwing one into the water, and then had to deal with a boatman who was frightened of storms on the lake although there were avenues between the reeds offering protection from the wind. At Bandipur he had no difficulty in hiring ponies for transport as it was the jumping off point for supplying the important garrison of Gilgit, a major post on the Silk Road, along which Buddhism had spread from South Asia to the rest of Asia. Gilgit sits on the main route into the Karakorum and Himalaya Ranges. In 1877, in order to guard against the advance of Russia, the British India Government, acting as the suzerain power of the princely state of Jammu Kashmir, established the Gilgit Agency. The Agency was re-established under control of the British Resident in Jammu and Kashmir.

John's party consisted of several "shikaris" or hunting guides, a "tiffin coolie" as cook and a "khitmutgar" who performed part of the duties of a footman; he prepared the table for the various

meals, and waited at table, afterwards cleaning the plates. After a stiff uphill walk of 23 miles over the Tragbat Pass, John sat down to a dinner of 5 courses. He had very poor Hindustani but carried a text book with him, and as none of his hired help spoke English, his diary was his only companion. His second night on the road was spent in a mountain hut where he even managed a hot bath and found traces of gold in a nearby stream.

At Gurais he ran into several intrepid ladies riding ponies with strong accompanying parties; they were so well turned out that he recognised the need to smarten up a bit on the trail. This was timely as the next day he met the Count of Turin, Vittorio Emanuele of Savoy, a prolific international hunter who slaughtered in his time the usual copious quantities of wild animals, including elephant and tiger. The Count also stayed in the hut and as John commented "I don't expect he often gets an eight penny hotel bill". His father had become King of Spain briefly in 1870 through a vote of the Cortes and he won fame for a duel with swords in 1895 with a French Prince who impugned the honour of the Italian Army, winning after 5 reprises after he had seriously wounded his opponent. He was commander of the Italian Cavalry in the First World War.

John picked up a couple of wires at Gurais and even wrote and posted a letter to his sister Amy, such were communications under the Raj! At Patchiwali he ran into an officer called Davy from the Gloucester regiment who had been hunting for two months and had 5 head of Ibex. At Minemarg there was only one European in place who managed the telegraph station monitoring the Gilgit wire; John observed that he produced wonderful photos on Velox paper. A telegraph maintenance party had been recently wiped out by an avalanche in the nearby mountains. After Minemarg the mountains became bleak and it blew and it snowed all night. The following day was not much better as his party climbed up 2000 feet to cross over the Doesai plateau covering 25 miles before John went to sleep with all of his clothes on, three blankets on top and four below. The march across the plateau took place in driving snow as they reached a pass at 15,000 feet. As they descended a glacier, two ponies fell into a crevasse and as John was not thinking straight, he followed them, falling ten feet. It was easier to extract him than the animals. Before reaching Skardo village, the party ran into an abandoned pony carrying a load of almonds.

John had not washed for several days and had splitting headaches because of the altitude but he could not resist having a shot from his tent at 7 wild mountain sheep crossing the mountain opposite, 220 yards away and 300 feet higher. He had no luck. At Skardo the plateau was around 4 miles wide and seemed to have any number of rivers crossing it. He thought that he had got a great deal buying apricots but it turned out when he bought a sheep that he found that he had vastly overpaid for the fruit. The horses were sent back from Skardo and he continued with "ten coolies, who were a queer crew", one unfortunate having to carry his tent weighing 100 lbs. The hike out of Skardo was quite tricky as the party crossed the Indus River, went for 6 miles over the hills and then re crossed the river again. They then arrived at Shigar where he pitched his tent on the polo ground and had a long chat with a Maharajah who was comforted by the presence of 30 wives.

John organised a game of foot polo with local children who played some wonderful strokes. He called on an English padre who was running a local school with the support of two English ladies. A Major Hibbert had been hunting for 5 weeks and bagged nothing. The party set off again following the Indus which flows north at this point, making a crossing that took 5 hours to get everyone over through using a raft of 24 pigskins which had to be inflated by mouth. As they zig zagged along the Indus, the raft had to be blown up and deflated several times. They finally reached a nullah, or deep valley, where John intended to hunt and immediately set off for a 4,000 foot climb into the snow in search of ibex which were seen but were just out  of range. He was exhausted and had a big headache as they pitched camp, but drank a large hot whisky and went to bed.

On Sunday 3rd September, John emerged from his tent to chase 30 Ibex and then saw a snow leopard in pursuit of the same prey. Fortunately for the leopard, his first pounce failed as if he had killed an ibex he would have hung around and made himself vulnerable to getting shot. John had something of a soft heart however, as one of the chickens who had been brought along as live provisions took a fancy to him and liked to roost in his tent and call him in the morning; John resolved to take the chicken with him back to Sialkote.

The diary gives a good flavour of the character of John at this time; "Monday 4 September. I have had another ripping day. I set out at dawn and went to our old hiding place and began to play the game of sitting still and looking at the Ibex through glasses. After about 2 hours of this I was sick of it, I was either going to kill or lose the beasts. They were on the other side of the valley, about 2,000 feet up – we were at the same height on the ridge. We could not go up because of the snow in the mountains; we could not go down to the Indus because that was impossible, so we slid directly over the ridge and dropped onto the glacier. Then the Ibex became suspicious so we lay flat on the rocks for an hour and jolly cold it was. I decided to make an actual dash for it across the glacier, leaving behind my shikari and carrying my own gun and shoving a few biscuits in my pocket. This caused my chaps great distress as it was a gross breach of custom to leave them behind. It is not that I particularly want to kill things- although the horns are nice, but it is difficult to explain the attraction of this activity. If the same keenness were necessary to take a photo of the beast, I would take photos only."

"Well, I set out across the glacier at a run and at once took a terrific fall on the ice, dislodging a stone which set about 40 million roaring down the nullah. I lay quite still until I really could not stand them any longer, then I made another bolt for it and got across under cover of a huge cliff. I crawled up this and then found a shot impossible and couldn't get any further without being seen – so I waited. In half an hour, the shikari came up and soon after a snowstorm came on - we dashed up under cover of this like rabbits to a spot about 150 yards from where the Ibex had been – but when the snow cleared, they had gone, or rather were disappearing fast. I could not resist the temptation and fired, hitting at least one badly but he staggered away - they can go as much as 300 yards before falling. We could not follow because of the storm. So we returned to camp, 2,000 feet down the glacier, 2,000 feet up, and 2,000 feet down again. It was dark before we hit camp - the last mile was steep, like Folkestone Cliffs and we took some beautiful tosses in the snow".

It appears that once Ibex are spooked, they will not return for ten days or so which meant moving to a new nullah. The weather turned nasty with heavy rain below and snow on the tops. The campsite was weather bound and even the Deosai plateau was closed. John found the Kashmiri guides difficult to fathom- they worked hard and seemed resistant to pain from falls and cuts etc. but were easily intimidated. His temper was not helped to discover that his cook had placed a whole unopened tin of haddock in the fire to warm up, creating a glutinous mix of fish and solder. Through his Bury telescope, he could see from his tent another European struggling up a mountain about 8 miles away – he enjoyed the vicarious pleasure of watching him climb.

On September 7, the day before his birthday, the weather was perfect and so he climbed a new nullah with his team but the only Ibex he saw were too small to hunt, so they descended and began their return home. After overnighting in a hut used for sheep in winter which had no chimney, he was delighted to be caught up by a shikari that he had left behind to trail the ibex that he had wounded earlier, bringing in the heads of two Ibex - one with 42 inch horns and the other with a 40 inch spread. He recorded that he could have shot a number if Ibex on the mountain that day but saw no need. "There are two ripping glaciers in this nullah which meet just below. Coming up we passed several warm springs. The shikari had forgotten his humble- bubble and tobacco so after lunch, I gave three of them some of my tobacco. They got a stick and laid it on the ground; they then scraped mud over it, patted it down and carefully withdrew the stick. This left a sort of little tunnel; at one end they pushed in my tobacco, lit it and then smoked it through the hole in turns. It was a bit gritty I am sure, but such is the devotion here to my Lady Nicotine."

"September 10. Got back to camp when dark and got a wire. The Regiment is ordered to hold itself in readiness. Return at once. Hooray! Hooray...When the deuce will it dawn. Dear old Kruger!!" (Kruger was the Boer President who kicked off the war)

With news of a possible war in South Africa, John embarked precipitately on his return to Sialkote moving fast over ground that he had previously covered at a more moderate rate. John's enthusiasm is not difficult to understand in a young man who just turned 22 on 8 September and who joined the Army to see action. He covered in two days the distance he had done in four and on 13 September he walked 43 miles over the Deosai plateau, having picked up baggage ponies at Skardo. He was really worried that he would get left behind but still could not resist a hunting opportunity.

"About 6 this evening, I saw a huge black bear right up on the mountains, I only had a Mauser pistol and 6 cartridges but I thought the stalk too tempting, so away I went, and got within 60 yards before he saw us and went off at a great pace. I had two shots with my stupid little pistol and they both hit - he stopped, got up on his hind legs and scratched himself as though a mosquito had bitten him. The shikari observed that the bear only had contempt for the small pistol."

As he trudged along keeping a close eye on the narrow path, thoughts raced through his head. Was it all a false alarm, would he be left behind, would he see any decent fighting, was the Regiment already embarked? At Minemarg, with access to the telegraph, he caught up with all of the news which gave further stimulus to the march so on 10 September he covered 67 miles from the Borzil hut through Minemarg and Guran Gurai, over the Tragbat pass to Bundipore, starting and finishing in the dark.

There is a despairing note in John's final entries in his diary which indicate his state of mind. "We sail Monday week. I am in an awful mess. A lot of baggage and a lot of hired stuff are in Skardo. My servant coolies are scattered with sore feet all along the line of march. I am going to Sialkote to pack up. I don't know where a single thing is. I don't know what I shall do with my bungalow things; I had begun to furnish it for your (Amy's) coming out. I have got three ponies that I don't want now, and I have not got the two chargers that I really need. I honestly think that I will be left behind. I have only led my troop on parade about 6 times and have done no scouting or reconnaissance at all."

John need not have worried - he embarked with his troop for South Africa to pursue the next phase of his adventurous life.

Chapter 7

War in South Africa

The Regiment had received orders to embark on 8 September 1899 (John's birthday). All officers on leave in India were recalled, 86 time expired NCOs and men voluntarily extended their services and with the addition of a few men from the 4th Dragoons and the 11th Hussars, the Regiment was up to war strength. The 5th left Sialkote in 4 special trains en route for Bombay; it consisted of 18 officers and NCOS and 476 men each with their Squadron horse. Each officer was allowed three chargers and in addition there were machine gun horses (one gun was allowed per regiment). At Deolali, B and C Squadrons had to be kept back temporarily because of contact with horses suffering from anthrax at Sialkote and so D embarked alone for Natal. The 5th were allotted the transports Patiala, Verawa and the Lindula, D Squadron departing on the latter. These ships were immensely uncomfortable; the men had cabins on and below the waterline with the horses above and the officers around and on top of the stalls. After a very rough crossing from Bombay (one ship lost 95 horses) the Regiment arrived at Durban on October 11th. The 5th survived a severe storm but departed one day after arrival for Ladysmith. The journey on a narrow gauge train up a climbing and twisting gradient was something of a nightmare for the tightly packed horses.

There were very few British troops in South Africa at the outbreak of the war, except in Natal where there were two

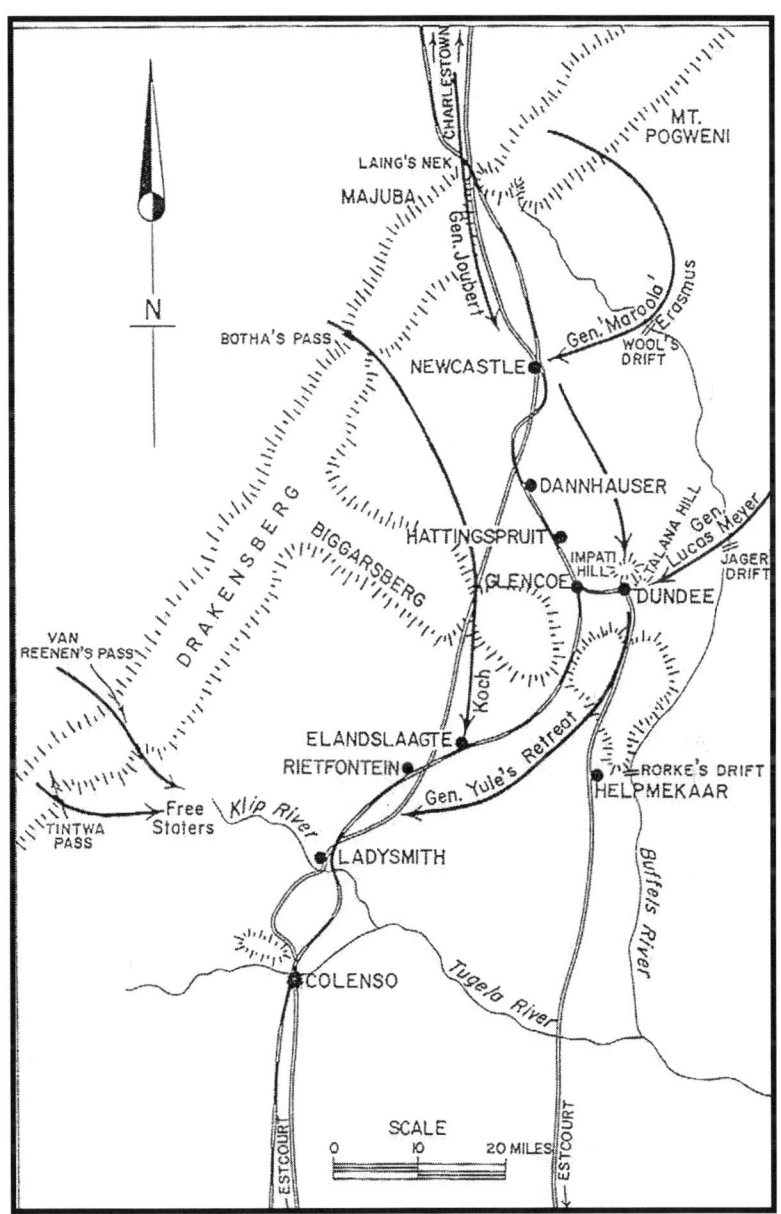

Cavalry Regiments and about a Brigade of Infantry with Artillery and Departmental troops in proportion – certainly not more than 7,000 including a small number of Volunteer Corps, for example, the Imperial Light Horse recruited mainly from the mines on the Rand. In Britain, an Army Corps and a Division of Cavalry of around 50,000 men had been mobilised but they would not be at the Cape before the end of October at the earliest. Whilst the long term prospect for the Boers was not promising as they would never be able to field more than 50,000 men, their best chance was to strike a decisive blow before the bulk of the British troops could intervene by smashing the Natal Field Force. To accomplish this, they entered Natal by Laing's Nek from the Transvaal and through Van Reenen's Pass for the Free Staters. Their adversaries by this time consisted of about 4,000 troops under Sir Penn Symons at Dundee and 8,000 at Ladysmith under Sir George White. The strategic significance of Ladysmith was that it lay at the junction of the two railway lines and thereby blocked the supply lines for any further incursion south.

White was in a rather difficult position as unless he could defeat the Boer Force ranged against him which would grow exponentially in numbers, he had to hold his ground and wait for relief in the knowledge that the correct strategic advance against Pretoria was via Cape Colony which with its three harbours and three railway lines rolling across open country was obviously the correct line of approach for a force whose great advantage lay in its numerical superiority. Conversely, the approach to Pretoria from Ladysmith constituted a logistical bottle neck, especially in view of the narrow defile of Laing's Nek which guarded the entrance to the Transvaal.

Action began on October 16 when Joubert and his Transvaalers appeared on Talana Hill above Dundee making the British position untenable. The British attacked at once and drove the

Boers from the hill but Penn Symons was killed, the British failed to shell effectively the retreating enemy and a Squadron attempting to cut off the Boers found themselves with no choice but to surrender. Colonel Yule, now in charge was ordered to fall back on Ladysmith. Meanwhile, Baden Powell, who was a Dragoon, was busy organising the defence of Mafeking having been ordered to South Africa after home leave from India.

There was an element of inevitability about the Anglo Boer war which derived from the clear incompatibility of British and Boer interests in South Africa and the failure of both sides to reconcile them. This had already lead to war in the 1880s which ended with three British defeats culminating in the humiliation of Majuba Hill in which the Commander of the British Forces perished with a large body of his own men as a consequence of his own incompetence. The defeat ended a brief period of British annexation and allowed the Boers to regain their independence, leaving the British with loose claims of suzerainty. The discovery of gold on the Rand and the arrival of British and other "outlanders" to mine it, together with the imperial ambitions of people like Jameson and Rhodes, threatened peace by challenging the dominance of the Afrikaner culture in the Boer republics of the Transvaal and the Orange Free State. The ill - fated attempt by Jameson to "invade" the Transvaal from Bechuanaland to link up with an anti-Boer rising in Johannesburg proved catalytic. Jameson was captured and imprisoned and the Boers refused to accept British denials of complicity. Talks lead to nowhere until, strengthened by the support of a dominant Afrikaner party at the Cape, President Kruger demanded the withdrawal of all British troops from the Transvaal border and the removal of all reinforcements.

The ultimatum was rejected and on 12 October, the Boers crossed into Natal - the war had begun.

The military centre of gravity at the outbreak of the war was Natal as this was where the main British garrisons were concentrated. The British needed to hang on to Natal whilst reinforcements arrived from overseas. Conversely, if the Boers were to succeed, they needed to deliver sufficiently crushing blows to dissuade the British from continuing…..they were encouraged, erroneously as it transpired, by the outcome of the first war with Britain in which the disenchantment of the public with the war had played a part in promoting an early settlement. They invaded Natal in three columns, arriving quickly in the vicinity of Newcastle. As we have seen, Penn Symons decided to ignore a suggestion from his military superior, General White that it might be more sensible to retire to Ladysmith rather than fight, and paid the price. The battle of Talana, named for the hill outside of Dundee on which the Boers were ensconced, was at best a pyrrhic victory for the British who suffered heavy casualties - 500 as compared with 150 Boers. Their column then retreated to Ladysmith.

Whilst Talana was in progress, the right hand column of Joubert's force under General Kock swung into the settlement and small railway station of Elandslagte, where a train was captured and a concert held in the local hotel. Defences were somewhat desultorily constructed on hills to the south and south - west of the station. In Ladysmith, 17 miles to the South, White realised that the Boers would have to be dislodged if the retreating column from Dundee under General Yule was not to be cut off. He appointed General French (later to take charge of the British Expeditionary Force in France in 1914) to command the 3,500 troops assigned to the task. The infantry consisted of the Devonshires, the Manchesters and the Gordon Highlanders; there was also Field Artillery and two squadrons of cavalry, including one of the 5th Dragoons in which John Norwood was serving.

The battle began with a preliminary exchange of artillery. The infantry were then sent forward under the command of Colonel Ian Hamilton who was brave, good looking and immensely popular (unlike his namesake, Brigadier General Gilbert Henry Claude Hamilton, of the 14th Hussars who is harshly criticised by John Norwood in his diary - they served together in later campaigns). He gave a rousing speech to send everybody off in good spirits and away the infantry marched across open grass plain keeping a yard apart until they were 900 yards from the Boer lines. The subsequent action was described afterwards in the Times as seen from the Manchester's lines.

"As we crossed the skyline, we were met by a perfect hail of bullets and the Gordons began to reinforce us. The men had all thoroughly got their blood up by this time, and they went at the hill in splendid style. It was steep and broken with rocks and stones. As we went up it, we saw the Boers gradually begin to leave their Sangers and retire. Then our own drums sounded the charge and it was taken up by the Gordon's Pipers, and we dashed in with tremendous cheer. Very few of them waited for the bayonet".

At this point, after the Boers were defeated and the survivors attempted to flee the scene on horseback, the Cavalry were released and engaged in probably the first full - blooded charge since the Crimea. The charge is most prosaically described by Colonel Gore who was in command of the 5th at the time.

"At 5.20 p.m. the enemy were seen coming out of their position into the open plain, and taking a line of retreat in the direction of Glencoe. I then gave the order to advance. My two Squadrons were formed in line as extended files, and charged across the line of retreat the enemy were taking. The latter were going away quietly at the trot,  until our men's heads appeared over the crest of a hill; they then changed their direction and galloped away in front of us from all directions. Their ponies were no match however for our horses and we rapidly overhauled them. Those men who tried to escape were attacked with lance and pistol and those who jumped off their horses and threw down their arms were made prisoners, unfortunately, it was now quite dusk, and it was extremely difficult to see where the enemy were. The first charge was from a mile and a half to two miles in length. The two squadrons were then halted, faced about and reformed. Then they charged back again over almost the same ground, and encountered a good many more of the flying enemy."

The Dragoon Guards had sharpened their swords and lances in India and the experience of being at the receiving end of a

Cavalry charge of about 200 men must have been truly terrifying, particularly as some of those run down might have been on foot. In the USA from whence many volunteers to the Boer cause had come, sections of the press embarked afterwards upon a campaign of vilification, drawing upon stories of excess brutality from letters from survivors (many of then Irish Americans). Elements of the British press followed suit, indelibly staining Elandslagte with the image of Dragoons slaughtering small parties of terrified and helpless Boers. As one Irish American wrote; "the Lancers acted as if fighting Indians and gave no quarter, stabbing and murdering prisoners and wounded in a terrible fashion, just like a lot of Sioux. It is said that the officers are responsible for this dastardly work, but it makes little difference to us. That lot of gentry are down in our black book and if the opportunity presents itself - and I know it will since there are some of them in Ladysmith - we will wipe that regiment off the rolls."

John Norwood's account of the battle does not corroborate the wilder versions of events. His experience is recounted in a letter to Gore that was published in "The Green Horse" in 1900 and dated Laing's Nek, September 4. 1900.

"Dear Colonel, I intended writing to you yesterday, but had to go out for a 40 mile patrol, and in consequence had no time to do so. Major Hensay told me on Sunday that you wanted an account of my personal experiences at Elandslagte.

On my way out from Ladysmith, I and my troop were acting as advance party to the advance guard, and it was not until just before we got to Modder Spruit that I knew there were any Boers about. However, when we all halted and the General was seen with a telegraph operator tapping the wire, we soon heard that there was every possibility of a fight.

On moving off again we felt our way along the west side of the railway, Reynolds with Sergeant Harris scouting the extreme left, whilst Travers and his troop were on our left front. We had not gone far before they found the enemy, and as I watched some hundred or more Boers clean missing at short distance a whole range of mounted cavalry, a pet theory of mine fell to the ground and I realised with keen satisfaction that the Boer was by no means the shot that I had always considered him to be. Under the persuasive influence of a battery of Artillery, these Boers soon quitted the kopje that they were on, and we advanced once more.

Just as the ground was becoming near impossible, Captain Mappin came over with an order from you to go to the other (East) side of the railway. Directly we crossed over, I could see more or less how things had developed. The real Boer position could be seen - their artillery was unmasked and artillery duels proceeding. Our infantry were just beginning to deploy, and I soon saw that we ourselves were being slowly but surely worked around on our left flank to the right rear of the Boer position.

Apparently, about this time the Boer gunners also came to the same sage conclusion, and thinking to prevent it, gave us the full benefit of their guns. As soon as the ground west of the railway allowed, you will remember that you sent us across the railway again, and we cantered to the colliery under heavy shell fire, and another pet idea of mine - that a shell on bursting killed everything for twenty yards around - again tumbled to earth. On reaching the colliery we waited and watched the fight, full of wonder how men could live in such a fire

.

Four or five times when the musketry rose to an absolute and continuous roar, some said the assault was taking place, until at last we saw a thin but ever increasing line of Boers begin to escape from the rear of the assault and position, and then we realised that our chance was coming. At last we set off. It had been raining and we were wet through. Personally, I had on a mackintosh, and a black cardigan vest tied around my neck - a splendid charging kit for a dragoon! We soon got into line and went away - left shoulders - and we had them right across our line.

Of the rest, I have the very vaguest recollection - a vision of Watson cocking his Mauser; a crowd of Boers with their hands up and their arms cast away.

Meantime, I steadily let off my Mauser, until my eye caught a Boer on a white horse getting away, so I pursued but Wynne of the 5th Lancers caught him first with a nasty sword cut over the head; then I saw another Boer and stupidly went after him, but couldn't catch him. On turning around, I could just see the squadron on the skyline a mile or more away. By the time that I got back it was quite dark and they had gone, so I wandered around to see if I could find or help any of our wounded. There were a lot of Boers lying about, but no English.

To one Boer I offered brandy but he refused it, murmuring something like..."poison". Then I met Panchaud with Sergeant McCormick, six men and about a dozen prisoners, and we tried to make our way back. However, it was such a pitch dark night that it was impossible to move, so we took off the horses bits to stop them champing, tied up our prisoners in a lump, and stood - to in a donga all night. Our reason for doing this was because someone said that the troops had gone back to Ladysmith and that Elandslagte was again in Boer hands.

It was a beastly night, cold, damp and no rations, and I was rather surprised to see the men give up coats and blankets to the prisoners -some of whom were wounded. At about 2

a.m. we heard horsemen, and by lying down could see them circling round and round us, evidently trying to find out who we were. We challenged and two men promptly bolted, but three other came in and gave themselves up, and as one had a bottle of whisky with him, he was greeted with effusion. It dawned at length, and we found ourselves in a donga about three miles northwest of the station. Great was our relief on getting to Elandslagte, that the place was still in English hands."

Such is my experience of Elandslagte. I fear that it is very feeble and won't be of much use to you. I see in my diary that I have written only the following -
Elandslagte,
Cavalry Scouting

Artillery Duel
Infantry Advance
Infantry Assault
Cavalry charge and pursuit
Lost myself and spent the night on the veldt. Probably the
prettiest day's fighting I shall ever see."

The battle ended with about 400 casualties on both sides. The
Red Cross helped to clean up the battlefield and the British
Forces then trekked back to Ladysmith, the key point that
they had to hold if they were to stand any chance of
reversing the tide of war. The illustration shows a somewhat
fanciful version of events.

After the withdrawal from Glencoe and the battles of Talana
and Elandslagte, the total British troops concentrated in
Ladysmith amounted to about 13,500 men. Any idea of
retreating further south was discounted by concern that
this would amount to a signal to the Zulu to rise up.
Defending Natal from the line of the Biggarsberg Hills to the
north of Ladysmith was untenable because they lacked water
and were too far north; the Boers would have simply
outflanked them and fallen on Ladysmith. Retreat to the
Tugela River was out of the question because public opinion
in Britain would never have accepted the surrender of the
town with its 60 days of supplies, substantial arsenal and
key location astride the railway. White concluded therefore
that Ladysmith had to be held with a view to occupying the
Boers and preventing them from invading Natal further. His
strategy was to make attacks on Boer positions wherever
possible and to retain the largest number of the enemy in
place until a relieving force arrived.

Chapter 8

Winning the Victoria Cross

By 30 October, the British were surrounded by around 15,000 Boers whose ponies were tethered on the reverse slopes of the hills surrounding Ladysmith. Whilst the Boers were busy bringing up artillery to fire down into the bowl, White decided to launch a reconnaissance in force, first at Lombard's Kop where he hoped to inflict a crushing blow on the Boers and secondly at Nicholson's Nek. White's plan was to lead off with an attack by a major formation, designated the 3th Brigade consisting of 5 Battalions of Infantry and supporting Artillery, all under the command of Colonel Grimwood. Their purpose was to dislodge Lucas Meyer's Commandos from Long Hill, some 5 miles to the north - east of Ladysmith. In the meantime, a second column designated the 7th Brigade, containing 4 Infantry Battalions, Cavalry and Artillery under Colonel Ian Hamilton, were to contain the Boers on Pepworth Hill to the north. In addition, a third column of two Infantry battalions and Artillery under Carleton was to make a 7 mile night march to Nicholson's Nek, to hold the position securely for the Cavalry who were intended to pursue the routed burghers after the success of the two main British thrusts.

The British proved themselves to be woefully inexperienced at moving large formations about the veldt under cover of

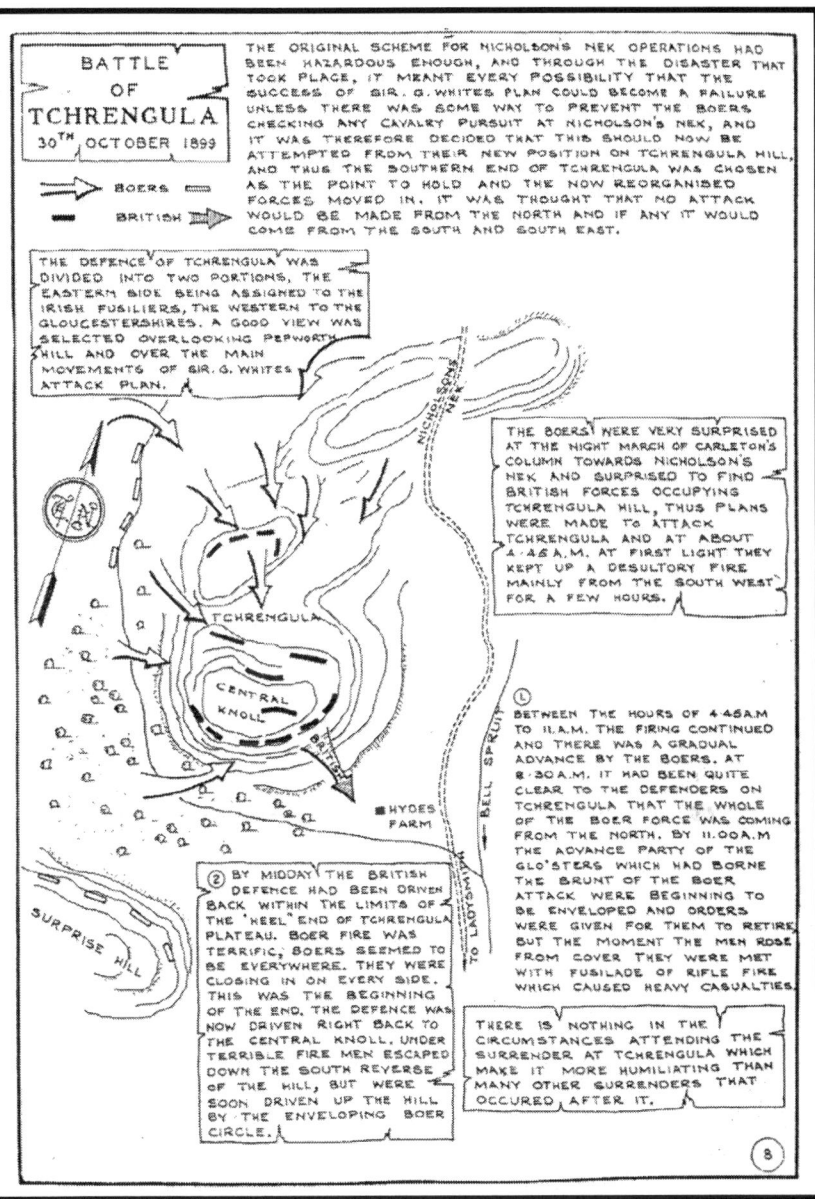

BATTLE OF TCHRENGULA
30TH OCTOBER 1899

→ BOERS ⇒
▬ BRITISH ⇒

THE ORIGINAL SCHEME FOR NICHOLSONS NEK OPERATIONS HAD BEEN HAZARDOUS ENOUGH, AND THROUGH THE DISASTER THAT TOOK PLACE, IT MEANT EVERY POSSIBILITY THAT THE SUCCESS OF SIR. G. WHITES PLAN COULD BECOME A FAILURE UNLESS THERE WAS SOME WAY TO PREVENT THE BOERS CHECKING ANY CAVALRY PURSUIT AT NICHOLSON'S NEK, AND IT WAS THEREFORE DECIDED THAT THIS SHOULD NOW BE ATTEMPTED FROM THEIR NEW POSITION ON TCHRENGULA HILL, AND THUS THE SOUTHERN END OF TCHRENGULA WAS CHOSEN AS THE POINT TO HOLD AND THE NOW REORGANISED FORCES MOVED IN. IT WAS THOUGHT THAT NO ATTACK WOULD BE MADE FROM THE NORTH AND IF ANY IT WOULD COME FROM THE SOUTH AND SOUTH EAST.

THE DEFENCE OF TCHRENGULA WAS DIVIDED INTO TWO PORTIONS, THE EASTERN SIDE BEING ASSIGNED TO THE IRISH FUSILIERS, THE WESTERN TO THE GLOUCESTERSHIRES. A GOOD VIEW WAS SELECTED OVERLOOKING PEPWORTH HILL AND OVER THE MAIN MOVEMENTS OF SIR. G. WHITES ATTACK PLAN.

THE BOERS WERE VERY SURPRISED AT THE NIGHT MARCH OF CARLETON'S COLUMN TOWARDS NICHOLSON'S NEK AND SURPRISED TO FIND BRITISH FORCES OCCUPYING TCHRENGULA HILL, THUS PLANS WERE MADE TO ATTACK TCHRENGULA AND AT ABOUT 4.45 A.M. AT FIRST LIGHT THEY KEPT UP A DESULTORY FIRE MAINLY FROM THE SOUTH WEST FOR A FEW HOURS.

TCHRENGULA

CENTRAL KNOLL

■ HYDES FARM

BELL SPRUIT

TO LADYSMITH —

(L) BETWEEN THE HOURS OF 4.45A.M TO 11.A.M. THE FIRING CONTINUED AND THERE WAS A GRADUAL ADVANCE BY THE BOERS. AT 8.30 A.M. IT HAD BEEN QUITE CLEAR TO THE DEFENDERS ON TCHRENGULA THAT THE WHOLE OF THE BOER FORCE WAS COMING FROM THE NORTH. BY 11.00 A.M THE ADVANCE PARTY OF THE GLO'STERS WHICH HAD BORNE THE BRUNT OF THE BOER ATTACK WERE BEGINNING TO BE ENVELOPED AND ORDERS WERE GIVEN FOR THEM TO RETIRE, BUT THE MOMENT THE MEN ROSE FROM COVER THEY WERE MET WITH FUSILADE OF RIFLE FIRE WHICH CAUSED HEAVY CASUALTIES.

SURPRISE HILL

(2) BY MIDDAY THE BRITISH DEFENCE HAD BEEN DRIVEN BACK WITHIN THE LIMITS OF THE 'HEEL' END OF TCHRENGULA PLATEAU. BOER FIRE WAS TERRIFIC, BOERS SEEMED TO BE EVERYWHERE. THEY WERE CLOSING IN ON EVERY SIDE. THIS WAS THE BEGINNING OF THE END, THE DEFENCE WAS NOW DRIVEN RIGHT BACK TO THE CENTRAL KNOLL, UNDER TERRIBLE FIRE MEN ESCAPED DOWN THE SOUTH REVERSE OF THE HILL, BUT WERE SOON DRIVEN UP THE HILL BY THE ENVELOPING BOER CIRCLE.

THERE IS NOTHING IN THE CIRCUMSTANCES ATTENDING THE SURRENDER AT TCHRENGULA WHICH MAKE IT MORE HUMILIATING THAN MANY OTHER SURRENDERS THAT OCCURED AFTER IT.

(8)

darkness. Grimwood lost half his force in his approach to Long Hill, as they followed the artillery to a different objective. The Boers had also slipped away and of French's cavalry, there was no sign. But as the dawn rose, Louis Botha's Commando of around 4,000 men were well placed across the stream known as the Modder Spruit to send a withering fire into Grimwood's flank. White was now obliged to use Hamilton's force to support Grimwood and by mid-morning the 8th Brigade had to be withdrawn to Ladysmith to avoid defeat. They were saved by rolling fire from the Field Guns who covered each other in alternate retirements.

Carleton's force had set off the previous night devoid of maps, but assisted by a local man called Mr Hyde who owned a farm at the foot of Tchrengula Hill. They went northward along the Bell Spruit towards Nicholson's Nek. The night was moonless and the terrain rough - conditions not altogether familiar to the men from Cork and Bristol who made up the majority of the force. On arriving at the Tchrengula, Carleton decided to occupy the hill to its north which overlooks the Nek to the north - east. As the force laboured up, a mule dislodged a rock and the noise alerted a Boer piquet on the top that opened fire wildly. The men were ordered to lie down, and when the piquet dashed through their ranks in the dark, the mules were startled and bolted, taking with them mountain artillery, shells and most of the force's ammunition. The Gloucesters and the Irish Fusiliers were left with only 20 rounds per man. The parlous nature of the British position only became clear as the sun rose.

Carleton found that, contrary to his intention, he was surrounded on all sides by hills taller than the one that he occupied and that the Boers were entrenched all around.

Sangers of stone were rapidly built, but the troops were cruelly exposed to Boer sharpshooters holding the high ground who could fire at will from behind rocks into their exposed position. The British lost many casualties, but in the end the battle terminated in farce. An outlying British platoon surrendered, the Boers took this for victory and emerged jubilant from their cover. Carleton, aware of his hopeless position and unwilling to fire on men who had revealed themselves, decided to surrender also, taking with him 37 officers and 917 men. It was all over by midday.

The fate of Carleton's force was clearly a matter of concern to General White once it became clear that the main thrusts had failed. The 5th Dragoon Guards were paraded at 3.30am and sent out to rendezvous with other troops at Limit Hill at 4.30 a.m. preparatory to finding out what had happened, against a background of artillery duelling between the two sides. The despatch subsequently written by Captain Hoare, the Commander of D Squadron to Major Gore tells the story.

"Sir, I have the honour to report the conspicuous gallantry of Second Lieutenant John Norwood and No 3720 Private William Sibthorpe, 5th Dragoon Guards, both of D Squadron, this morning during the action. While the Regiment was under cover of Limit Hill this morning, the officer mentioned was ordered to take his troop and examine and find out the position of the column (Note; Carleton's force) that were sent out last night to take a position on our left flank in the vicinity of Walker's farm. Owing to the proximity of the enemy at Bell's Spruit, who fired on him, he tried another line; this was unsuccessful, so he attempted another. This

was also unsuccessful, so he attempted another more to the north - west towards Smith's crossing. Here he was met by heavy musketry fire, and ordered his troop to retire; during the retirement, Second Lieutenant Norwood was in the rear of his troop, and on No 5439 Private Mouncer, who was hit by a bullet in the throat, falling from his horse, he dismounted and picked up the wounded man on his back, and began to walk in with him. Private Sibthorpe hereupon returned to Second Lieutenant Norwood's assistance and assisted in carrying the man.

No 3352 Sergeant Harris of the same troop, having got the men under cover, returned to assist Second Lieutenant Norwood and Private Sibthorpe; the wounded man was put on Sergeant Harris's horse. They were under heavy fire from the enemy who were on the side of the hill about 400 yards off. The wounded man was left with a piquet of the 19th Hussars who were on the north - west of Limit Hill, I believe that the officer in charge of this piquet witnessed most of this, but Lieutenant Norwood could not give me his name.

On his return to the Regiment Second Lieutenant Norwood reported his failure to General Sir George White, but it was not until Private Sibthorpe's gallant act had been reported to me by his officer, Second Lieutenant Norwood, that I knew anything about this officer's part in it, for on my talking to Private Sibthorpe, he remarked "He only followed his officer's example". I then questioned Sergeant Harris mentioned above; he corroborated Private Sibthorpe's description of Lieutenant Norwood's act. This officer informed Sir George White that if he would allow him to take his troop dismounted, he thought that he could get well into the valley and perhaps accomplishes the object that he was sent out to attain. He was ordered to re-join his regiment.

It is against the express wish of Second Lieutenant Norwood that I reported his share in this act of gallantry.
I have the honour to be, sir,
Your obedient servant, H Hoare, Captain Commanding B Squadron, 5th Dragoon Guards"

Gore then wrote the following letter to DMG Cavalry Ladysmith, for the information of the GOC Cavalry Division; "I would wish to recommend most warmly Second Lieutenant John Norwood and No 3720 Private William Sibthorpe both of the 5th Dragoon Guards, for the highest honours of a soldier, for their gallant action in bringing away a wounded comrade out of the trap in which they found themselves. Dated Ladysmith, I November 1399."

John was awarded the V.C. and Sibthorpe the Distinguished Conduct Medal. The war artist Melton Prior who we met before at Abu Klea was at Ladysmith and captured the moment for the Illustrated London News in a drawing which he gave John and with which he is forever associated. This is still with the family. John had nothing negative to record about his CO, "Fruity" Gore, as he was known in the mess. Gore was something of a martinet who did much of the talking in the mess and usually showed marked reluctance to listen to others. Mouncer, a shoe smith, appears to have survived his experience and later entered civilian life.

The trap around Ladysmith was still closing, but there was nothing inevitable about the siege until White decided after the reverses of what the press described as "Mournful Monday" to stay and fight. It was never in the Boer's thinking to assault the town directly. It now held around 14,000 effectives (including locals) defending entrenched positions with artillery and maxim guns. By the first few days of November, the Boers encircled the town almost completely, occupying more or less static positions on the outer ring of hills, notably Pepworth, Long, Gun, Bulwana, End, Rifleman's Ridge, Telegraph and Surprise Hills. This perimeter was about 6 miles in diameter, providing a platform for Boer artillery about three miles from their targets in the town. This artillery consisted of some fairly large guns, including the famous Long Toms, hurling 96lb shells from a 6 inch barrel, 12 pounders and 37mm howitzers. The Boers confidently expected the British to realise that their position was hopeless and to sue for terms.

The British on the other hand, were simply waiting for Buller to come and relieve them. Both sides went through the motions of making war in the meantime; the British sent out sorties to test Boer reactions and the Boers rained in shells. The British infantry were strung out along a rise of inner hills, reinforced by the Navy's 4.7inch guns on Junction Hill, a couple of howitzers and a few batteries of Royal Artillery guns. After the last train for Maritzburg successfully escaped, a census of the town revealed 13.500 military, 5,500 white citizens and 2,500 Africans and Indians.

The two adversaries were not unevenly matched in numbers, but they had very different attitudes to the conduct of war. The Boers were an undisciplined citizen force, patriotic and totally committed but unschooled in the notions of military command, submission to strategic plans which were not visibly and dramatically intelligible, or the need to submit personal viewpoints to the authority of an untried stranger. One Boer commentator observed that "Foolhardiness on the battlefield is forbidden; no Boer thinks of risking his life merely from a superfluity of courage. Such rashness is rewarded by censure, for every man who falls deprives his family of a breadwinner and weakens his commando and the prospect of victory".

The British private was described in 1895 by Lord Wolsey as

"the worst paid labourer in England". Ignorant, and for the most part feckless and lacking in imagination, the average British recruit of the day was only semi - literate at best, and not even a robust specimen. One county regiment could only muster 370 fit men out of 950 for overseas service in 1899. Even before the outbreak of war, it had been necessary to reduce the statutory height norms for recruits below the standards of 5ft 3 inches for infantrymen and 5ft 5 inches for cavalrymen established in 1897. In addition, the British infantryman was poorly trained and his recent experience limited to colonial wars against crudely armed tribesmen. The Crimea in the 1850's was the last war fought against a European Army. Most training since had been limited to annual manoeuvres of about three weeks during which about 220 rounds were fired in volleys.

Gore writes in "The Green Horse" that "Our men can shoot capably at a target, at a known range and with officers who themselves know the range to tell them. The Boer is just the reverse. Each man is capable of doing all this for himself; he shoots with his head; the first question he thinks about is "What is the range?" Consequently, he can be put into a sanger all day by himself with a bag of cartridges and shoot at any mark that presents itself in the knowledge that he will use his head". The 5th Dragoons decided to emulate this characteristic; they were given extensive practice with infantry rifles, told to ignore the manual of musketry regulations and simply select targets and ranges themselves by eye. They were soon amazed by the accuracy that they were able to achieve....and not before time.

The one quality expected above all from the British Army

however was bravery. There was in particular a cult of reckless bravery among the officers, especially the Cavalry, which drove them to pursue military glory at almost any cost. Their code of conduct regarded the defiance of danger as wholly honourable. Deliberate self exposure to risk demanded no clear vision of military advantage. This thinking is amply demonstrated in the diaries of John Norwood and arguably contributed to his eventual death in France. The courage of the rank and file was of a different order. They seemed to possess a profound and often seemingly invincible fortitude, and an almost infinite capacity for accepting suffering and discomfort without complaint. They appeared to be sustained by notions of imperial grandeur and an unswerving commitment to the exercise of military virtues that was to be brutally tested in the major war ahead.

After the disasters of Mournful Monday, the 5th Dragoons were mustered to form part of the mounted troops held as a central reserve near White's HQ on Central Hill under Major General Brockenhurst. They soon found themselves a place on the left bank of the Klip River about a quarter of a mile above the Poort Road where it ran through a small defile. Here trees gave shelter from the view of the Boer gunners if not from their shells. The bivouac was named Green Horse Valley after the distinctive dress uniform of the regiment and splinter proof shelters were constructed and a photograph was taken of the officers showing John standing at the extreme left.

The Dragoons Maxim gun was posted at the north end of Observation Hill under Lieutenant Melvill. For the next couple of months, the camp received regular shellfire, which frequently failed to explode on impact, which is just as well as

there were several narrow escapes. One shell skipped over Gore's head, another missed the Medical Officer by a yard and stopped in Platt's unoccupied bed. Yet another passed between the MO and his patient Captain Gaunt before exploding. Matters improved after the successful attack on Gun hill on S December when a Long Tom was blown up with a breech charge. Life was only rendered tolerable however when a watch was set to observe gunfire and blow a warning whistle which gave everyone about 20 seconds to find cover; the shelters were also dug deeper. But the horses could not be protected and lack of forage took its toll. Men began to die of enteric fever at the hospital at Intombi, positioned with Boer agreement in neutral territory close to the Boer lines on the road to Colenso.

The Boer attack on Wagon Hill and Caesar's Camp which

commanded the flat topped ridge to the South - East of the town was the only offensive infantry action by the Boers during the siege. It took place on the night of 6 January when several hundred Free Staters poured on to Wagon Hill in the glare of their own search light. The hill became a confused mass of fighting men, the British holding the position tenuously as a consequence of having built a small fort on the top. At Caesar's Camp, the position was different as the defences were feeble. The Transvaalers stormed the ridge and established a foothold on the crest; when the dawn rose, they were swarming all over the crest and they took the picket line of the Manchesters in the rear and cut them down in swathes. In the early morning sun, the field guns of the 53rd Battery trotted out and cleared the South - East slopes with shrapnel but neither the crest nor the slopes beyond could be reached. It was essential for the infantry to engage, and they did so at heavy cost.

By 7 a.m. over 2000 men on both sides were deployed lying flat in the firing position and separated in places by only a few yards of grassy hillside. Three British charges met with annihilation until at 1 p.m. the Boers broke their own rules and charged the Sanger at Wagon Hill, leading to panic before they were driven off.

By 4 p.m. it was clear that the Boer effort had failed; a tremendous thunderstorm broke over the field as the Devons were sent out to make a final charge across 130 yards of slippery grass at Wagon Hill. After one volley, the Boers withdrew and the action was all over. British losses of 424 men, of which half were killed, were greater than Colenso.

The 5th Dragoons had been ordered at 5 a.m. to act as

THE ATTACK ON WAGON HILL AND CAESAR'S CAMP
6TH JANUARY 1900

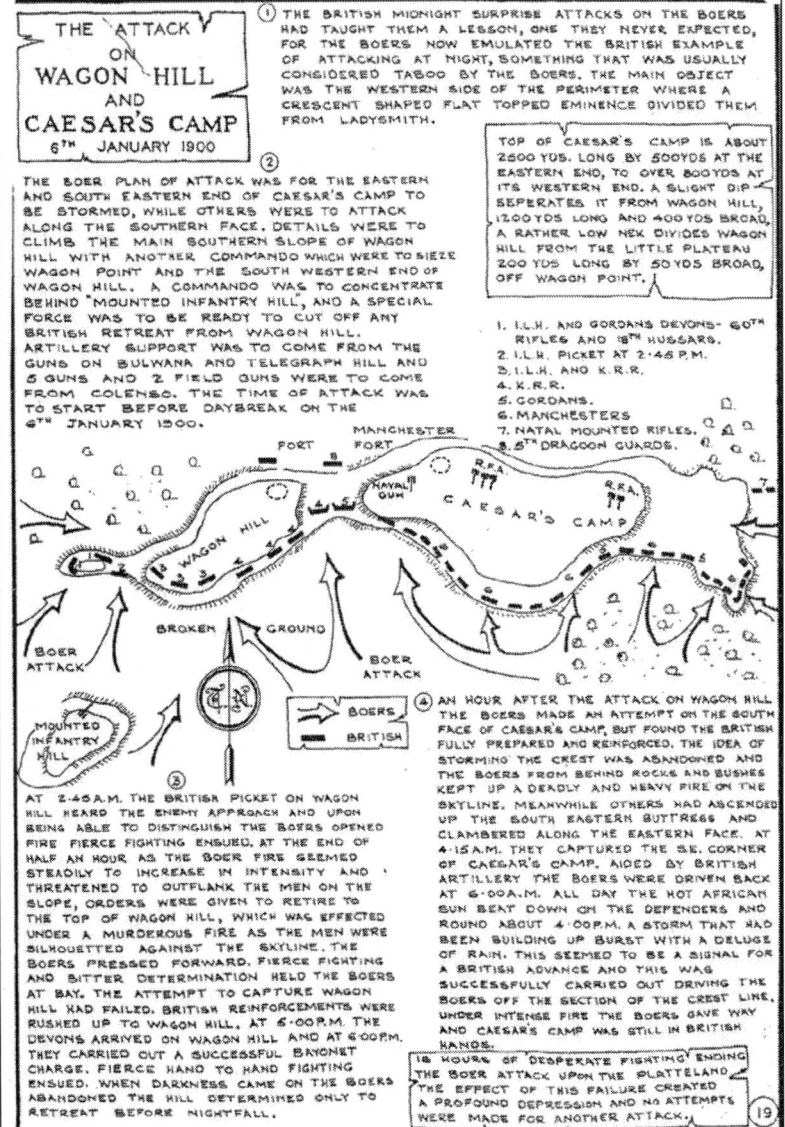

① THE BRITISH MIDNIGHT SURPRISE ATTACKS ON THE BOERS HAD TAUGHT THEM A LESSON, ONE THEY NEVER EXPECTED, FOR THE BOERS NOW EMULATED THE BRITISH EXAMPLE OF ATTACKING AT NIGHT, SOMETHING THAT WAS USUALLY CONSIDERED TABOO BY THE BOERS. THE MAIN OBJECT WAS THE WESTERN SIDE OF THE PERIMETER WHERE A CRESCENT SHAPED FLAT TOPPED EMINENCE DIVIDED THEM FROM LADYSMITH.

② THE BOER PLAN OF ATTACK WAS FOR THE EASTERN AND SOUTH EASTERN END OF CAESAR'S CAMP TO BE STORMED, WHILE OTHERS WERE TO ATTACK ALONG THE SOUTHERN FACE. DETAILS WERE TO CLIMB THE MAIN SOUTHERN SLOPE OF WAGON HILL WITH ANOTHER COMMANDO WHICH WERE TO SEIZE WAGON POINT AND THE SOUTH WESTERN END OF WAGON HILL. A COMMANDO WAS TO CONCENTRATE BEHIND "MOUNTED INFANTRY HILL", AND A SPECIAL FORCE WAS TO BE READY TO CUT OFF ANY BRITISH RETREAT FROM WAGON HILL. ARTILLERY SUPPORT WAS TO COME FROM THE GUNS ON BULWANA AND TELEGRAPH HILL AND 5 GUNS AND 2 FIELD GUNS WERE TO COME FROM COLENSO. THE TIME OF ATTACK WAS TO START BEFORE DAYBREAK ON THE 6TH JANUARY 1900.

TOP OF CAESAR'S CAMP IS ABOUT 2500 YDS. LONG BY 500YDS AT THE EASTERN END, TO OVER 800YDS AT ITS WESTERN END. A SLIGHT DIP SEPERATES IT FROM WAGON HILL, 1200YDS LONG AND 400 YDS BROAD, A RATHER LOW NEK DIVIDES WAGON HILL FROM THE LITTLE PLATEAU 200 YDS LONG BY 50 YDS BROAD, OFF WAGON POINT.

1. I.L.H. AND GORDANS DEVONS- 60TH RIFLES AND 18TH HUSSARS.
2. I.L.H. PICKET AT 2·45 P.M.
3. I.L.H. AND K.R.R.
4. K.R.R.
5. GORDANS.
6. MANCHESTERS
7. NATAL MOUNTED RIFLES.
8. 5TH DRAGOON GUARDS.

③ AT 2·45 A.M. THE BRITISH PICKET ON WAGON HILL HEARD THE ENEMY APPROACH AND UPON BEING ABLE TO DISTINGUISH THE BOERS OPENED FIRE FIERCE FIGHTING ENSUED. AT THE END OF HALF AN HOUR AS THE BOER FIRE SEEMED STEADILY TO INCREASE IN INTENSITY AND THREATENED TO OUTFLANK THE MEN ON THE SLOPE, ORDERS WERE GIVEN TO RETIRE TO THE TOP OF WAGON HILL, WHICH WAS EFFECTED UNDER A MURDEROUS FIRE AS THE MEN WERE SILHOUETTED AGAINST THE SKYLINE. THE BOERS PRESSED FORWARD. FIERCE FIGHTING AND BITTER DETERMINATION HELD THE BOERS AT BAY. THE ATTEMPT TO CAPTURE WAGON HILL HAD FAILED. BRITISH REINFORCEMENTS WERE RUSHED UP TO WAGON HILL. AT 6·00P.M. THE DEVONS ARRIVED ON WAGON HILL AND AT 6·00P.M. THEY CARRIED OUT A SUCCESSFUL BAYONET CHARGE. FIERCE HAND TO HAND FIGHTING ENSUED. WHEN DARKNESS CAME ON THE BOERS ABANDONED THE HILL DETERMINED ONLY TO RETREAT BEFORE NIGHTFALL.

④ AN HOUR AFTER THE ATTACK ON WAGON HILL THE BOERS MADE AN ATTEMPT ON THE SOUTH FACE OF CAESAR'S CAMP, BUT FOUND THE BRITISH FULLY PREPARED AND REINFORCED. THE IDEA OF STORMING THE CREST WAS ABANDONED AND THE BOERS FROM BEHIND ROCKS AND BUSHES KEPT UP A DEADLY AND HEAVY FIRE ON THE SKYLINE. MEANWHILE OTHERS HAD ASCENDED UP THE SOUTH EASTERN BUTTRESS AND CLAMBERED ALONG THE EASTERN FACE. AT 4·15A.M. THEY CAPTURED THE S.E. CORNER OF CAESAR'S CAMP, AIDED BY BRITISH ARTILLERY THE BOERS WERE DRIVEN BACK AT 6·00A.M. ALL DAY THE HOT AFRICAN SUN BEAT DOWN ON THE DEFENDERS AND ROUND ABOUT 4·00P.M. A STORM THAT HAD BEEN BUILDING UP BURST WITH A DELUGE OF RAIN. THIS SEEMED TO BE A SIGNAL FOR A BRITISH ADVANCE AND THIS WAS SUCCESSFULLY CARRIED OUT DRIVING THE BOERS OFF THE SECTION OF THE CREST LINE, UNDER INTENSE FIRE THE BOERS GAVE WAY AND CAESAR'S CAMP WAS STILL IN BRITISH HANDS.

16 HOURS OF DESPERATE FIGHTING ENDING THE BOER ATTACK UPON THE PLATTELAND THE EFFECT OF THIS FAILURE CREATED A PROFOUND DEPRESSION AND NO ATTEMPTS WERE MADE FOR ANOTHER ATTACK.

19

MANCHESTER FORT · FORT · NAVAL GUN · R.F.A. · CAESAR'S CAMP · R.F.A. · WAGON HILL · BROKEN GROUND · BOER ATTACK · BOER ATTACK · MOUNTED INFANTRY HILL

BOERS — BRITISH

escort to the 21st Field Artillery and to accompany it to a position outside the line of defences to about a quarter of a mile from the range post, so as to prevent any Boers crossing from Mounted Infantry Hill to attack Wagon Hill. The Battery opened fire on Mounted Infantry Hill at 6a.m. surrounded by a screen of dismounted Dragoons, some in a nullah about 400 yards to the left rear of the battery, with one patrol out from the left of the battery to Wagon Hill and another patrolling up Flagstaff Spruit. Incoming fire was received from Middle and Telegraph Hills and Rifleman's ridge, forcing the Battery to withdraw to lower ground. Two shells fell in the nullah to little effect, beyond wounding Captain Darbyshire's horse ("Darby" was a good friend of John Norwood).

At 3 p.m. two Squadrons were ordered to Wagon Hill where they were dismounted and placed amongst rocks along the inner crest of the top of the hill so that they could sweep the level plateau with fire should the Boers show over the crest line. There they stayed until dark as insurance in case the Devons' charge failed. After dark, they were moved up to Wagon Hill to hold it during the night; Gore sensibly ordered his men to construct a line of defensive sangers (it was Hamilton's failure to do this at Caesar's Camp, together with his inexplicable decision to leave his men leaderless there whilst he charged off in pursuit of action at Wagon Hill that had helped the Boers make their initial advances). At 9 a.m. after both sides collected their dead, the Dragoons were sent back to Camp.

In the meantime, life for Darbyshire and his escort of the 21st Battery was not uneventful, according to his report; they were sniped at and shelled, some shot falling right in the   middle of the gun teams from the Boer guns on Middle Hill. After heavy rains flooded the nullahs in which both sides were concealed, the Boers decided to go home at 4 p.m. followed by the Dragoons at 7 30 p.m. after a decent interval. John Norwood's Diary offers his own reflections on the day; "An eventful day. I was awoken at 5 am. by shrapnel breaking over my tent. As I was orderly officer, I dressed roughly for ration inspection but just as I was leaving, the Supply Cavalry Depot orderly came up with an order for a regimental turnout and assembly at Gun Park. I was told off to take dismounted men up to Rifle Post but later on, to my great joy, Harris took my place and I set out to catch up the Regiment which had been gone some half hour. I went up to Caesar's Camp and Long Tom Umbulwana on the way up nearly wiped me out by bursting a shell only 5 yards behind my horse right in the middle of the road - the nearest squeak from this gun that I have yet had. I was sniped for about half a mile and arrived only to find not the 5th Dragoons but only the Manchesters fighting like steam. Deciding with wonderful promptitude that duty did not require my staying, I retraced my way to Range Post where I found the Noble Green Horse acting escort to Blewitts XXI battery and shelling steadily with 4 guns in position. This went steadily all day with wonderful luck to us 'til the rain came on at about 5 p.m."

"Darby, Punch (presumably Panchaud) Travers and self crawled out and did some quite ineffective sniping at 2000 yards at Boers who seemed to be massing for a fresh attack. Up to 5 we lay all day under guns from three sides and phutting bullets from Lord knows where. About 5, awful storms came on and curiously enough the fighting bucked at once. No reserves were to be had, so we left the battery with a tiny escort and went on to the   top of Wagon Hill. Myself with fellows mentioned above could not get back from our sniping, the dongo in the rear having become a torrent 30 foot wide, so we were stuck there. At about 8 o'clock the show quieted off, only a column of ambulances and moving lanterns everywhere telling the same tale of the ghastly day. Got back to Camp and was rubbed down by Dr Ville for half an hour, then Darby and I turned in after drinking our last half bottle of wine - I was very lucky to get back as the Regiment did not get in until noon on the Sunday morning."

It seems from this account that John Norwood and his colleagues became bored with escort duty to the Guns and attempted to join up with the Squadrons who had been detailed to hold the reserve line on Wagon Hill. This private excursion is tactfully omitted from the official report of Darbyshire.

John Norwood (seen washing in the Klip River) was admitted to Intombi hospital on 26 January with enteric fever, an ominous development. His diary recorded the death of Platt from enteric fever on 5 January at Intombi and the "Green Horse" is punctuated by regular death notices from similar causes. During the weeks remaining before the end of the siege, Major Heneage, Captain Darbyshire, Major Hoare, Captain Mappin and Second Lieutenants Kinner, Pomeroy, Melvill, Norwood and Watson all spent time at the hospital. It is clear that the group photograph of the officers at Green Horse valley must have been taken early in the siege as they all look quite healthy. John was in hospital from 26 January until 15 March. He recorded in his diary on 12 February that things were very bad in the hospital and that there were 10-15 deaths per day from "lack of luxuries"; his own temperature veered wildly.

Gore described conditions at the hospital on 11 February as follows; "The poor fellows are suffering a great deal from dysentery and enteric and intermittent fever. The cruel part of it all is that there is scarcely any of the all - necessary milk to give them, and they have to do the best they can almost upon the ordinary ration we are getting. Once a man gets into a weak state, it is difficult to pull him around again without giving him nourishing food. Of course all the tinned milk, whisky, brandy, arrowroot and everything that would be of value to sick men was commandeered, so they are getting all there is available. If Buller's guns are heard nearer, or if any good news is given to them, they cheer up wonderfully and say they feel better; but if they have bad news, or no news at all, the death rate is certain to be heavier on that day as much from sheer weariness and weakness from want of food, as from the diseases to which the deaths are attributed."

By this state in the siege, the rations consisted of half a pound of preserved meat or one pound of fresh meat, half a pound of biscuits or one pound of bread, one sixth of an ounce of tea or coffee, one and a half ounces of sugar and half an ounce of salt with a little pepper. The fresh meat was from the horses (see drawing below) and a hot soup called "Chevril" whose origin is obvious, became a staple diet. Already by January it became impossible to feed the horses so the majority were simply turned out to fend for themselves. The majority of the Dragoons became, in effect, dismounted infantry.

John Norwood's diary contains an important entry for 28 February 1900; "Went out, bed and all, for the first time. Saw relieving column coming in to the right of Pagwane - can hardly believe it". In the next few days, his temperature oscillated wildly, but in the excitement and relief "no one cares a damn". The sick and wounded at Intombi Gamp were indeed the first to spot Buller's column which had finally fought its way across the Tugela after bloody battles at Spion Kop and Colenso. After their last action in taking a row of hills to the south of Ladysmith which culminated in dislodging the Boers from Pieters Hill on 27 February, the Boers were allowed to retreat by Buller unimpeded. His forces were exhausted after two weeks solid fighting which was just as well for the Boers whose leaders privately acknowledged that they would have collapsed if attacked.

The consequences of failing at Ladysmith however had been fatal to their cause. From Ladysmith they could have moved on to Durban, the only major port in Natal, whose seizure would have enhanced the possibility of foreign intervention on their side as well as made the prospect more daunting for Britain of landing quickly and safely the large numbers of troops that were required to turn the tide. As it was, their retreat brought the era of set - piece battles almost to close. The Boers turned increasingly to guerrilla warfare, which lead to reprisals, anti- guerrilla "drives" and the establishment of concentration camps. The writing was on the wall for the Boer cause.

Chapter 9

An Invitation from Queen Victoria

As for John Norwood, he was scarcely in a fit state to enjoy the parade and celebrations. He records that some patients at the hospital became sick from over - eating and by 9 March, he was able to potter around the Camp on an orderly's arm. The first train left for Colenso on 10 March and he was passed fit to go South on 13 March; he wrote on 15 March; "Left Intombi Hospital - Thank God!" By 16 March he was ensconced at the Hotel Ocean View in Durban. His illness nonetheless continued to plague him; it was hot and he was unable to keep food down. His friends were due to sail on the SS Gascon, but he had difficulty in getting approval from the medical board to travel. He finally obtained 4 months leave on 27 March and received permission to take the Gascon if he could catch her. He noted, "Needless to say, I packed in time to do this and 5.30 saw us leave on time".

The SS Gascon which was built in Belfast in 1897 and was new to the Cape route was carrying 13 officers and 150 men. The first few days were rather rough, making it necessary for John to be shaved in bed, but later there was whist in the Captains cabin, quoits and lazy days. The boat arrived in Tenerife on 16 April and the officers lunched at Taraconte on the road to Oratava; the island was pretty and new passengers boarded, causing John and friends to moderate their behaviour; Diary entry "21 April; a very pleasant voyage. Captain Chope, Foster (R A) Warre and self played bridge daily. Wigan and I ragged all day. Up to Tenerife we smoked everywhere and did what we like. After picking up ladies, we had to behave. Lady Slacke and Mme Cunninghame were the best of a very poor lot." Frances Rose Slacke was the second wife of Captain Sir Owen Randal Slacke of the 10th Hussars and she was already on the boat having visited her husband in South Africa.

John was met at Southampton, where he moved overnight into the Great Western Hotel, by sister Amy and a bevy of friends. It seems that their London home was 41 Oakley Street. His life in London was a whirl of theatres, clubs and dining out at the best of places. He was a member of the Carlton and the Cavalry and a regular at the Cafe Royal, He also took in the Savoy and the Trocadero. He saw "London Courage", "The Rose of Persia" (from a box at the Savoy), "The Messenger Boy" at the Gaiety, "San Toy" at Daleys, "The Rivals" at the Haymarket, "A Messenger from Mars" (starring the well-known actor manager Charles Hawtrey), "Cyrano de Bergerac" at Wyndhams and also went to the Alhambra. He played a lot of cards and usually ate out after the theatre.

Amy was John's constant companion. On 16 May they took the train to Eastbourne and stayed at the Grand Hotel. Some friends called the Simpsons were also down; it was a "ripping cold day" and he and Amy walked on Beachy Head in the morning and rode in the afternoon. After another ride on the following day (16 May), he heard that Mafeking had been relieved. The day after he biked to Hailsham (where coincidentally his daughter-in-law subsequently lived) to see the Maguires and the Melvilles (probably the family of JL Melvill whose family came from Sussex - he was invalided home and never returned to South Africa). His diary also mentions Lillian Collen, his future wife.

John had to see his dentist, Mr Blum on his return to London and was invited to dinner. The experience was not entirely agreeable as he met there a "violent pro- Boer", provoking the reaction in his diary of "Ye Gods preserve me!" He called at the offices of the family firm in the Borough High Street and lunched at the George in Southwark with Arthur Wolton.There were bicycle rides to see friends in Highgate (the Patons) and to Regents Park, Ewell and Malden with Amy. Finally, on Naval Brigade day (7 May), he saw a Mr Goodhart at the War Office where he was pronounced fit to return to South Africa. He wrote "Hooray!" in his diary, packed his bags and left Oakley Street on 23 May to take the 9 30 am. from Waterloo for Southampton where he sailed with the SS Britannia at 2.30 p.m. He was sea-sick as usual.

Whilst in Oakley Street John received a letter from the Queen's Equerry which read; "to Lieutenant J. Norwood, 5th Dragoon guards, co Miss Norwood, 41 Oakley Street, Chelsea (Invitation to Osborne).

"Sir, I have to acquaint you that the Queen has been pleased to signify her gracious intention to personally confer upon you the decoration of the Victoria Cross early in the week commencing 20th instant. The exact date and hour will be notified to you in a further communication. "

It appears that John did not attend Osborne to receive his award which would have had to be brought forward, as he was soon en route to South Africa. Queen Victoria died in the following year before he could return.

The voyage to the Cape was uneventful; the boat contained about 1060 men and 60 officers. Most of his companions were judged "excellent chaps", including a Roman Catholic padre called Rawlinson, and Guards officer, Cave-Brown to whom he lost thirteen pounds ten shillings at piquet. He bought a table clothe for Amy at Las Palmas, was impressed by whales off West Africa and was amused by the discovery of 6 stowaways who had deserted after being declared unsound for military service and had then smuggled themselves on board the same boat as their regiment. The boat arrived at Capetown on 10 June. John lunched a great deal and enjoyed meeting two officers from Buenos Aires, Captains Dominguez de Larrinaga and Fair. He mixed with the mighty, dining with Sir P Chichester and then sailed via an overnight stop in Simons Town to Port Elizabeth, participating there in a singsong with an Australian boat load of volunteers. Each boat sang songs alternately, including "Australia for the Australians and England for us all". The Australians disembarked and marched ceremoniously through the town.

John sailed on to Durban, enjoying the fine weather, to be met there by his Aunt Ellen and his cousin Una whom he had given away to Charlie Adams of Eshowe when they married in October 1899 as after he made a brief foray from Ladysmith down to Eshowe and back before the Boer net closed on the town. (The Adams wedding had taken pace just two weeks before the action in which he won his VC.) John's stay with his relatives at the Belgrave Hotel in Durban was comparatively brief.

The connection between the Adams and Norwood families is of some interest. Alfred Adams was born in 1841 in West Maidstone Kent and went to Africa in 1860 with the Universities Mission to Central Africa to assist Bishop Mackenzie to establish a mission in the neighbourhood of Lake Nyassa and the Shire River (a marker showing the site of the mission is said to exist near the main Zomba-Blantyre Road in Malawi). The guiding light of this enterprise was Dr Livingstone who helped to transport the original party of thirteen missionaries up the Zambezi and its tributaries to their first settlement at Magomero. Livingstone's idea was that if a regular system of agriculture and commerce, growing cotton and coffee etc., could be introduced into Africa, the slave trade could be overcome. He had substantial public support and the Government sponsored this adventure, giving him the title "Her Majesty's Consul at Quelimane"

All participants, including Alfred whose official title was "agriculturalist" experienced great privations and disease, suffering from fever, dysentery and hunger as crops failed. Alfred had good knowledge of the countryside however, a strong constitution, abundant enthusiasm and a good sense of humour. As he sat in the farewell service in Canterbury Cathedral, he little knew that he would need all of those qualities. Livingston's rosy view that the Shire highlands were fertile; abounded with game and enjoyed a healthy upland climate may have appeared true from the Kongone mouth of the Zambesi where he awaited the party's arrival, but was wrong. After a preliminary encounter with malaria, requiring a short period of rest in the Comoros, the expedition headed up river on the paddle steamer Pioneer. The boat ran aground frequently, requiring packing and repacking of cargo - it took two months to reach the highlands and Magomero, where they constructed a rough settlement, Livingstone now departing again for the coast. Apart from disease they now had to contend with hostile tribes and slavers. Their community was swelled by freed slaves but their supplies dwindled, their crops proved insufficient and even a move to a new site failed to halt the deterioration. Surviving rough paintings show Alfred Adams, still in the thick of it, trying to keep the mission going.

Mackenzie died to be swiftly followed by six others; two women attempting to join the mission also died as did Livingstone's wife. Bishop Tozer took over but the conditions were too harsh and after another attempt to build a station at Morambala, higher on the plateau, the mission closed in 1864. Adams was the only survivor of the original team. He returned briefly to England to recuperate and was then sent to join the Reverend Robert Robertson who was running the first Anglican Mission to the Zulu at Kwamagwaza. Bishop Mackenzie's widow was instrumental in raising the money for this venture. On the boat to Durban, he met his first wife Selena Wood whom he married in 1868.

Robertson had established a good relationship with Mpande the Zulu King but was demoralised by the death of his wife who was crushed by an overturned supply wagon as they returned to their mission from Durban. Alfred set to work enthusiastically and supervised the construction of the first brick church requiring the manufacture of 60,000 bricks. Whilst initially, Zulu converts to Christianity were cruelly killed, gradually small groups joined up and eventually King Mpande gave formal consent to this process. Adams also started a cattle endowment scheme which was intended to make the church self- financing and which after 5 arduous years provided Alfred after his contract ended with the knowledge to set up as an independent farmer on land given to him by King Mpande on the north bank of the Tugela about 8 miles from its mouth. John Dunn, a famous and quixotic adviser to the Zulu added a school and mission to the settlement to the site which became St Andrews - it remained in the hands of the Adams family until in 2003 it was sold to become an agricultural training site for local farmers (many of whom traced their ancestry to Dunn who was a polygamist).

Although Cetshwayo, who succeeded Mpande, was on good terms with the missionaries themselves, and often had serious discussions on religion with them, in the following years, relations between the British and the Zulu deteriorated and in January 1879, British troops crossed the Tugela to invade Zululand, passing through St Andrews. In the years since Selena's death, Alfred had lead a peripatetic existence acquiring extensive first-hand knowledge of Zululand and getting involved in the transport business. He now joined with the British force and participated in the battle of Gingindlovu and the relief of Eshowe. After the defeat of Cetshwayo, Eshowe became an important garrison and administrative centre, so Alfred secured the contract to supply the garrison and opened a store in Eshowe in 1881 which grew into a major business and remained in family hands for virtually a century. However, he also restored St Andrews which had been ravaged by the war. In 1874 Selena gave birth to Charles

 Adams, but died two years later.

Towards the end of 1883 Alfred married again. His second wife was Elizabeth Best from Durban but sadly, like her predecessor, she did not live long and was buried at St Andrews in 1886. His third wife was Ellen Norwood, known to the family as "Auntie Nell" who he had met during a visit back to England. Ellen was a certificated teacher living with her mother in Edmonton North London in 1881 so was 41 at the time of their marriage in 1887 in Wynberg, Capetown. They probably met through Christian circles in London. To please his new bride, Alfred purchased a large piece of land in Eshowe where he built the family home called "Norwood". It was a spacious wood and iron house surrounded by verandas, standing in a large well-tended garden bordered by trees. (Around 2000 the wooden house was moved and installed at the Eshowe museum at Fort Nongqayi). Ellen was the sister of John Norwood, the hop merchant and the aunt of John Norwood V.C.

The connection between the two families is however more intimate still. Alfred's son Charles was brought up in Durban by his grandmother, Naomi Wood after his

mother died. After an apprenticeship to general merchants, he returned home in 1892 to take charge of his family's business. In 1897, his step mother Ellen, invited her niece Una Brown from London to visit the family in Eshowe. Una was the daughter of Kezia Norwood and Harry Brown.

Kezia, Ellen and John Norwood senior were of course the three children of Richard Norwood and Sarah Elizabeth Booker. Una was a tall, well-built young woman who suffered with chest trouble and it was felt that the climate would improve her health. It did more than that - Una and Charles Adams rapidly announced their engagement and after Una made a brief visit back to the UK in 1899, the wedding took place in Durban on October 12. Una had studied at the Slade and was quite artistic. The informal photograph of "Auntie Nell", John Norwood, Una and Charles Adams on this occasion is one of the few non-official pictures of John that now exists. Oddly, there appear to be no photographs available of the wedding itself.

Alfred Adams had a restless energy and apart from his store and transport business, he built a mill and bottled mineral water plant, opened butchery in Eshowe and still loved to trek on trading expeditions into Zululand where his former relationships with Mpande and Cetshwayo were well known. He died in 1906 in the middle of the Bambata rebellion and is buried at St Andrews on the Tugela, leaving his business to his son Charles.

Ellen Adams nee Norwood returned to the UK about three years later. The Browns were linked in both kinship and business with the Norwoods. Joseph Brown married Lucy Billing in 1843; they had three children, Walter, Harry and Lucy. The last two married brother and sister, i.e. Kezia and John Norwood. The Browns came from Hampstead and Finchley in north London and the business links appear to have developed through Brown's involvement in the haulage trade; there is some evidence that he was in partnership with a Henry Bourner who was mainly concerned with the carriage of hops in Kent. The 1911 census for 25 Temple Street Brighton finds Ellen living comfortably in a boarding house alongside Elizabeth Bourner, also the widow of a successful entrepreneur.

Whatever their origins, the links between the Browns and Norwood family became very close as the wills of John senior, and John and Amy Norwood testify. Indeed Amy (married name Coldridge) left more personal possessions in her will to members of the Brown family than to the family of her brother John. He in turn had left his medals to his sister and other military memorabilia rather than to his wife which seems odd in the circumstances.

Chapter 10

Return to Action

John was lodged in Pietmaritzberg in the Imperial Hotel on June 22, recording cryptically in his diary the name of a Mrs Murray Simpson. On the following day he rejoined the Cavalry Depot and began to get his eye back in by shooting at buck with the same lack of success as before. On 26 June he arrived back at Ingagane to resume the war. The Dragoons were now brigaded with the Royals with responsibility for guarding lines of communication, particularly the western side of the railway to Pretoria (the Royals had the East). Patrolling was constantly being carried out so that daily there were some twenty patrols seeking contact with the Boers. This lasted until May 1901.

Life at the Camp in Ingagane was initially rather dull. John played football and dined with the Devons, shot a stork, replaced worn out saddlery and chased phantom Boers. On 21 July, he went down to the railway station to send a wire asking for some carrots and ran into Bayley of the XIII who told him that his V.C. had been gazetted. He noted laconically in his diary, "Great Evening!". The Regiment was distributed in Squadrons between Kotzee's Drift, Ingogo. Laing's Nek, it's HQ at Volksrust and Zandspruit; John seemed to move between all these points, taking many photographs of the featureless veldt

which are largely unidentifiable. John was particularly taken with the site of the major British defeat in the first Boer War. "I rode all round Majuba and Laing's Nek, the Boer trenches etc.; this was most interesting and instructive" He later took photographs of General Colley's grave which together with other casualties is on the battlefield itself. Majuba is a very sombre and atmospheric place overlooking the entrance to the Transvaal which Colley must have believed was defensible but which was wholly vulnerable to an attacking force which saw its targets constantly silhouetted against the skyline.

John recorded in his diary the occasional reminder that life could be brutally short; "2 August; went out with 4 men to Moll's Nek, when lunching at Johnston Farm, heard firing. Found that Godson and 6 of our men had got scuppered". On 5 September, Hillyard with whom John rode frequently (they had just been to O'Neills farm at Majuba together) and a number of men were shot; Hillyard was taken down to Newcastle but died 7 September; John attended the funeral without comment. The Dragoons were going out on 40 mile patrols with occasional and unexpected contact; a few Boers surrendered under white flag, the railway was cut and on one occasion, an ammunition store containing 650 shells went up. The weather was frequently bitter, it rained and the wind sometimes masked the noise of very distant engagements. A diary entry reads "Not every man can go abroad to fight, perchance to die; but every man that wears a shirt can wear a khaki tie".

On 13 October, John was ordered to go to Pretoria. The problem was that the Boers had ambushed a train near Vlakfontein several days earlier. He finally made Pretoria on 10 October and was allowed to "slack about" for several days at the Eloff's farm before parading with others to receive the V.C. from General Roberts. Those similarly honoured were Phipps, Congreve, Fitzclarence, Gunner Lodge and Corporal Mackay from the Gordon Highlanders. He stayed at the Heaths Hotel in Jo'burg and dined with Panchaud and friends at the Cafe Royal before getting the train back to Laings Nek and riding on to Ingogo with Gage. In between escorting convoys to Newcastle and Utrecht, John seemed to be very welcome at the Moll's farm and at the Goodwin's. November ended with a brief flurry of action at Hurricane Hill in which about 150 Boers were attacked and bolted under fire. After Church parade on Christmas day, a gymkhana and sports were held for the men; John ran the rum tent and the day ended with a sing -song.

The final entry in the diary for 1900 is a snatch of verse;
"Do the work that's nearest though 'tis dull at whiles helping
  when you meet them, lame dogs over styles."

1901 was greeted with; "New Year. Hooray. Much more peaceful than last year but still not peaceful enough" On 23 January, the news of Queen Victoria's death reached the troops by heliograph from Laing's Nek. The situation on the ground was sufficiently threatening for John to sleep in a trench that evening, the danger perhaps explaining why he placed one of his men on a charge for neglect of duty. He records "Private Wilson shot his brains out at 5.40 a.m. after being placed under arrest by me at 3.15 a.m. for irregularities on guard." One must assume that the unfortunate sentry was caught asleep which presented a threat to the patrol bearing in mind the ubiquity of the Boers. Conditions on the veldt could be testing and according to the diary of Lieutenant E Collen, soon to be John's brother in law who was engaged in wagon escort duty, three of his men died from hypothermia one cold night.

Lieutenant Edward H Collen was an interesting character, having followed his father into the Royal Artillery; he soon managed to get himself out to India where he participated in frontier campaigns, such as Tyrah, which I have already mentioned. January 1990 found him in South Africa where he hoped to join the staff of Lord Roberts, the Commander of British Forces. Unfortunately for him, Robert's personal staff vacancies were full, so expressing regrets and apologies to General Collen, he was posted to a transport company. Whilst this seems unglamorous, in fact the function of getting supplies out to the troops was vital and required protection, Edwin saw a lot of South Africa and experienced arduous conditions but by the end of 1900, he was recalled to India. In the meantime, he kept an interesting diary and drew some evocative sketches of which the following are but a sample. John Norwood was a keen photographer but his pictures are less revealing than the drawings of his brother in law to be.

KERK STREET.

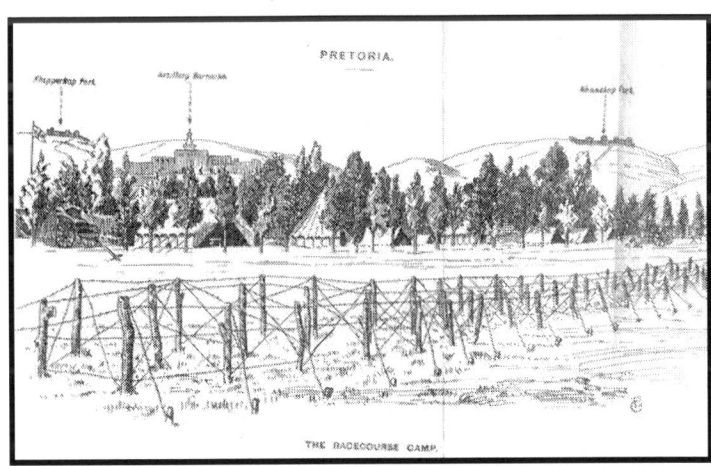

PRETORIA.

THE RACECOURSE CAMP.

THE GLEN.
18 miles from Bloemfontein.

BRIDGE OVER MODDER RIVER BLOWN UP BY THE BOERS.

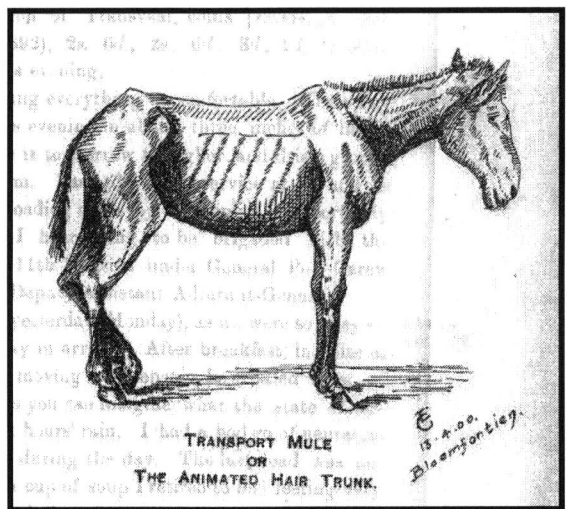

TRANSPORT MULE
OR
THE ANIMATED HAIR TRUNK.

Towards the end of January the Boers were very active and after a patrol from Alleman's Nek got into trouble, a troop was sent out in pursuit. John was down with toothache and had to make a quick trip to Durban for an extraction.

120

During the visit he managed to pack in "The Harbour Lights", a circus, "Oh Susannah" and "A Message from Mars"! (which he had already seen before in London with Charles Hawtrey).

February 1901 was a rather miserable month. The Dragoons were on escort duty, accompanying convoys to Utrecht. The wagons were often deeply mired; the drifts were flooded and Boer raiding parties much in evidence. John sniped at a party of 40 Boers near the Pwaan River on 14 February and then did a bolt. Doing flank guard and sleeping out on piquet did nothing to improve his humour. His man servant asked, in soaking rain, what he and another officer would like for dinner; the latter replied "soup, fish entree, joint, pudding and savoury" - " to our surprise this was seriously taken and duly delivered - how, I do not know". The patrol liberated some government protected sheep to extend their rations and John sought relief from the pouring rain by playing toss penny into a hat with another officer, and damming a stream. The troop was also providing protection for road mending and showed willing by building some fortifications to impress the visiting General Hillyard.

The troops were allowed to take booty and it is clear that getting hold of a wagonette with a hood to transport not only an officer's personal possessions but also to help carry the squadron's kit was a very desirable goal. These prizes were difficult to retain however, as they were always found eventually to be against regulations and confiscated. The regiment was hit hard on 13 March when forming part of a column that was ferrying supplies to General French in Piet Retief; Corporal Fagg and Private Wortley were killed whilst crossing the Mabiola Drift. It was difficult to provide all

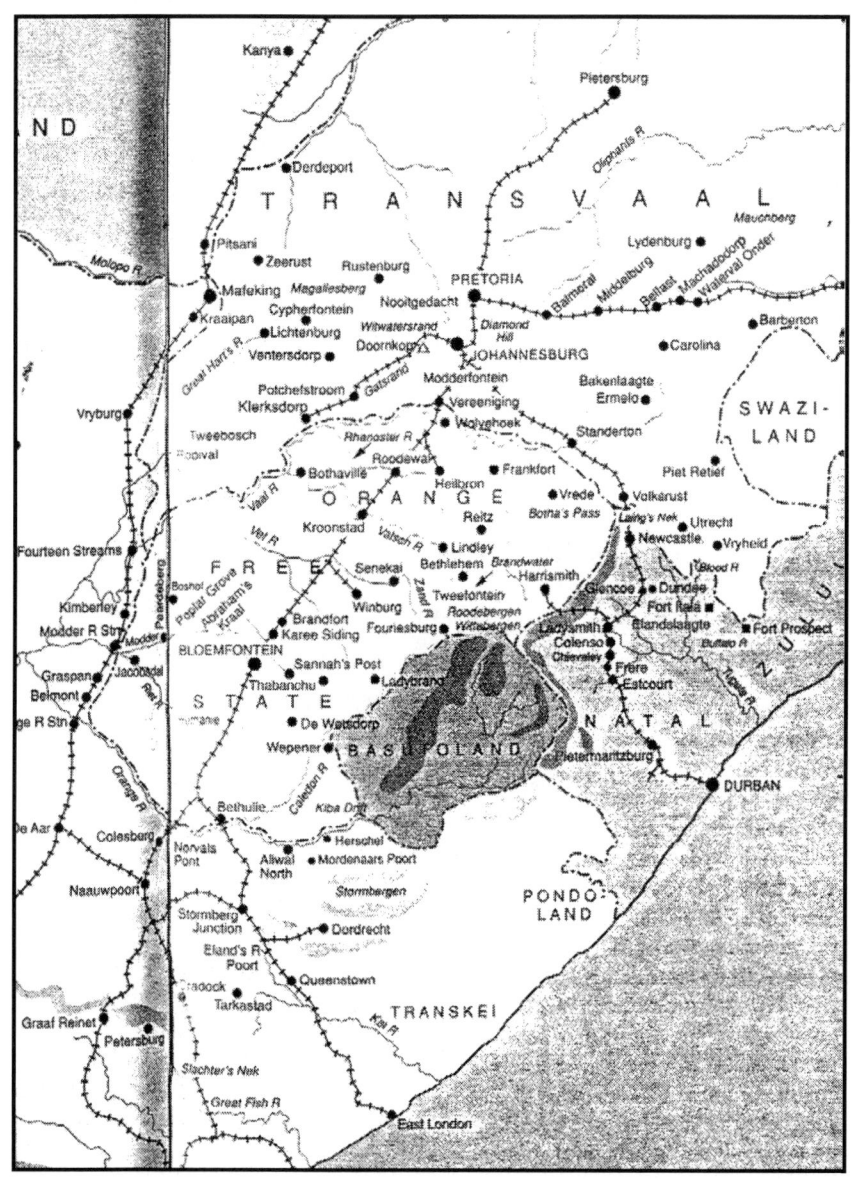

round protection as 500 odd wagons nearly extended over 17 miles even on good roads. As the map shows, the battlefield was widely extended and ever changing.

On May 1 1901 the regiment received orders to march to Standerton and on May 6 together with the 13th Hussars formed a Cavalry Brigade under General Gilbert Hamilton. John was delighted, writing that they had handed over an excellent mess and house to the VIIIth. They were now to take part in the final phase of the war. Their mission since the capture of Pretoria and the end of the conventional war was essentially to participate in the hunting down of guerrilla bands by means of cavalry columns whilst the lines of communication were held by infantry in blockhouses. Every now and then columns were united together with a view to driving some particularly notorious commander into a trap, such as De Wet…..but this usually failed.

The practice with mobile columns was to start from a supply depot, such as Standerton with provisions for ten days or a fortnight, to patrol a particular area and round up any commandos who might be in it. The idea was to collect intelligence on the enemies' whereabouts and then by means of a long night march, fall on them at dawn, leaving transport to follow. What generally happened was that the commando usually got away after a prolonged running flight, leaving families, sheep and transport abandoned in its wake. Everything captured then had to be marched back to join the column's own supply train, and then returned to depots to await further marching orders. Communication was maintained in the field by means of heliographs (a signaling device by which sunlight is reflected in flashes from a movable mirror), telegraph and despatch rider.

John met Jack Wigan, a son of one of the family business partners from the hops trade in Standerton. En route, he found the Klip valley fertile and full of buck. He visited Joubert's farm and admired its unusual private garden and cemetery. At Standerton the regiment was detached from the Brigade to work with Major General Elliot's force that was advancing on Vrede in the Orange River Colony, C and D Squadrons operating under Major Heneage joining Colonel Colville's column at De Laage's Drift on the left bank of the advance. John was critical of Heneage's leadership in one encounter with Boers, but seemed a little reckless himself when at Green Farm on 21 May; "I awoke at 4, and marched at 8 - as escort to the guns. I soon met Boers and had a very lively dust up. I couldn't get them off one kopje so went straight for it across open ground. Jerry up first, Sibthrope hit in lung" (the latter was of course Norwood's partner in the action at Ladysmith). He survived the war, became a coal clerk by 1911 and later a Chelsea Pensioner.

Afterwards, John again liberated some sheep, but was sniped so furiously by their owners, that he had to leave them behind. At Driefontein, he did flank guard and fought a rear-guard action all day, observing "they are good sportsmen these Vrede Boers". The same occurred on the following day; "These Vrede Boers certainly do fight like good 'uns. Had my horse killed under me by some 7 Boers who ambushed me; I lost the saddle and all but I was glad to get away". His dislike for his Brigadier was faithfully recorded; "Gilbert Hamilton is an incapable ass whose sole merit is that his brother is KK's private secretary." KK is Lieutenant Colonel Kekovich, a competent Cavalry commander who effectively brought the war to an end at the battle of Rooival in October 1902 killing the last effective Boer guerrilla commander, Jacobus Potgieter.

On 29 May the 5th Dragoons and 13th Hussars marched out of Standerton in Brigade and entrained at Greylingstad for Krugersdorp where they were to participate in the operations around the Magaliesburg. During an engagement with Dixons column shortly before they arrived, each side lost about 50 casualties. Krugersdorp was green and full of trees but the Dragoons were not there long. "Witwatersberg. Paraded 5.45 a.m. and went off to hold the Nek whilst Allenby's column works up the valley between Magaliesberg and Witwatersberg. I saw 40 Boer trekking away. On outpost all night with 30 men on the road through the poort...this is wild woody country, lots of owls screeching. I cut down a large tree to put down across the road." Later, he trekked on the flank of Allenby's column to Raalfontein and "saw one tame Boer who fled with even more alacrity than I could have done myself!" Two days later in a "nasty valley" not far from Raalfontein, the Squadron were ambushed and two men were badly wounded, Hill and Sinclair; the bullet passed through Hill's chest and emerged near his spine.

On the following day, the Dragoons burned out 30 farms in the area of Hartley's Tobacco Mill, and camped in the drawing room of the mill. Norwood's disenchantment with Hamilton (nicknamed Ghazi) comes through in another entry for 7 June; "Useless day. 7 Boers having fled from a farm that we were about to camp in, Ghazi became the brilliant general and galloped us a mile over stones, we halted and watered, galloped two miles uphill, halted 20 minutes, fed, went on one mile, turned back and got into camp about 5!!! And as we did not catch them, we doubled all outposts as a precaution.... Ye Gods!" More frustrating days followed as the Dragoons chased without success a wily Boer called Stroys and a column of oxen near Tafel Kop.

The Dragoons patrolled as far as Klerksdorp. Hartbesfontein. Stersfontein, Roorpoort and Ventersdorp. John walked rather than rode for some overnight stretches in order to keep warm and awake. An order arrived from Kitchener suggesting that more violence was required. This was not to John's taste...he burned down farms without enthusiasm; "This is rotten work, and I am very tired of it". He narrowly missed catching General Smuts at Lamoenfontein Farm; one of the sick Boer receiving treatment there under the Red Cross's aegis turned out to be a Boer despatch rider who was pretending to be ill. Near Wolmaransstad, some 40 Cavalry were ambushed and the survivors sent back without boots (and breeches in some instances) as was the Boer practice; they couldn't keep prisoners, but could use their weapons and clothing. On 26 July, after a night march, the column made a successful night attack on Potgeiter's Laager at Syfergat not far from Rustfontein. John was sent forward with the Dragoons as the advance guard and as dawn rose fell on the Boer party. The column captured 25 wagons, 1100 cattle and 4,000 sheep. In the melee a child was killed, to John's regret. "Ghazi was at first furious until the risk was over, then he smiled from ear to ear and forgot that the attack was done against his wishes."

The next period of operations involved a De Wet drive intended to capture the guerrilla leader. Hamilton's brigade formed part of the defensive line against which De Wet was to be driven, again without success. John heard whilst at Geduld on

5 August that the Regiment was to go back to India at the earliest opportunity. On the same day, he spent over an hour holed up in a Kloof under fire from 60 Boers. As if life was not sufficiently lively, however, two officers had a race around the outposts the following day for a sovereign. On the next day, the Squadron covered 51 miles in a cross country march to Moortgedaacht. More night marches followed.

On 15 August, Norwood passed by Vlaksfontein ... "the scene of Dixon's regrettable incident – there are huge graves – the action seems to have been a very serious one. The Boers very uppish here as is only natural. This is awful country; all kopjes and British graves". Brigadier General HG Dixon had been camping at Vlaksfontein as part of a search for hidden guns - but the information he received was false and his rear-guard was attacked, two guns seized, 49 killed and 130 wounded by a Boer force under Boer General Kemp of 1,500 guerrillas.

John had an interesting talk with a Basuto chief from whom he was buying equipment for the mess "He wanted to know what four prisoners were doing in our camp. We explained that they had put up their hands so weren't shot. He thought this was very stupid and said that when they put up their hands, then this was our chance (drawing a finger across his throat!)".This attitude is not entirely surprising as the Boers tended to be merciless to blacks who were suspected of being on the wrong side.

On 22 August after a 21 mile waterless march to Holfontein. "A curious dip in the veldt where a good stream suddenly appears and then disappears", John lost "Tum Tum" the last of his Indian horses, an Australian waler. Each officer had three chargers, one he rode himself, one was ridden by his first servant, who lead the third which carried his baggage. His second servant rode in the ranks and was mounted in the troop to which the officer was attached. After breakfast, Tum Tum was opened up and found "to have every disease under the sun". Over the next few weeks, John participated in extensive patrolling in the Nauwport valley, around Raalfontein and in the area of Oliphants Hoek and the Magaliesburg; camping on the top of the latter kopje at one point as part of a 100 man patrol under Kennard. Boers were fruitlessly chased and after dining with Wigan in Klerksdorp, John took a few days welcome leave in Jo'burg where he stayed at the Heath Hotel and dined with Panchaud, Mathias, Sir William Marriot and Chesney at the Rand Club. On 21 September, the Dragoons were taken by train back to Natal where they joined the rest of the regiment in Dundee, a town that John enjoyed, especially the Victoria Hotel.

On the move from Klerksdorp to Dundee the train in which the horses of C and part of B squadron were travelling became derailed between Paardekop and Standerton. 25 horses were killed and 40 injured; only 6 men received injuries and after the troops realised that it had been an accident rather than the Boers, those not engaged in cleaning up the mess, went back to sleep. On 27 September the Dragoons moved from De Jaeger's drift to Roode Kop where John noted "This is just near where Gough caught it".

Major Hubert Gough and a column of mounted infantry had been rushed down by rail from Pretoria to Dundee to deal with Botha's column that had invaded Natal. The British columns were exhausted by 20 months of scouring and sweeping the republics without success. Gough heard at De Jager's drift of the presence of around 700 Boers in the area and was delighted on crossing to the Transvaal side of the Buffalo to see some 300 Boers riding northward from the stony ridge called Scheeper's Nek, astride the main road leading to Vryheid. They off-saddled at Blood River Poort. Rather than wait for the arrival of a further 450 men held in reserve, Gough decided to charge the laager. Unfortunately, he did not see Botha's main force of 700 men who galloped around his right hand companies on a ridge and surprised his force on the open plain. In the ensuing fight, the British lost about 40 casualties and 240 soldiers were taken prisoner. It was the biggest humiliation since Nooitgedacht nine months before. Botha captured more guns and ammunition than he could use but the horses, his most pressing need were completely exhausted. He released the prisoners, having taken the clothing he required, and moved on.

Gough and the survivors joined the 5th Dragoons in Clements column. John spent Dingaan's day (23 September) on the Mabola plain. The threat from Botha by this time was disappearing fast as he made the grave error of attacking two well defended British forts, Itala and Prospect on 26 July which lead to heavy Boer losses and such demoralisation that Botha wrote " I must report that it was impossible for our men to enter Natal", he therefore retired to the Transvaal. The aim of his mission was in any event ill-conceived as 1000 men could scarcely threaten by this time the British hold on Natal. It was becoming clear to Botha that the choices were quite stark; to fight to the end or accept Kitchener's peace.

On 28 September, John accompanied guns to Rorke's Drift where he stayed near the mission station, observed Isandlwana (the scene of the devastating Zulu victory over Lord Chelmsford's force in the Anglo Zulu war) in the distance and crossed briefly into Natal before providing protection to road mending teams and escorting a convoy from Vants Drift. The Zulu were patrolling grimly the south east borderland, instructed by the British to repel any attempted invasion of their own territory. 5 October found John with General Clements en route to Nquta. He crossed the Nondwein River and moved through Spitz Kop to Bethe where he heard that his friend Jack Wigan had been breveted a major.

On 10 October the Diary records, evidently retrospectively; "Haven't kept a diary for this next month but we moved up northwards, trekking ail the time to Utrecht, W'strom and Volksrust. From there we were flung up by train to Standerton to go out to Colonel Benson's relief. Then back to Standerton and train to Pretoria where we arrived on 5th November." Resuming on 6 November, the Diary records "Arrived Pretoria. Good place, nice club and a good many hotels open. I saw the Chief. In fact, the Regiment was inspected by Lord Kitchener and received replacement equipment. It was thunderstorm weather, and several men were lost to lightning strikes."

The Regiment had made a forced march of 60 miles from Standerton in conjunction with the columns of Colonel Allenby and Colonel De Lisle to assist Benson. They arrived at Trigaardsfontein at 7 a.m. on November 1, but were too late to save Benson, who had been defeated at Bakenlaagte with loss of his guns on October 30, and had himself died of his wounds on October 31; but they were able to relieve the convoy and the remainder of the force who had entrenched themselves in

Nooitgedacht Farm under Colonel Sampson. The Boers dispersed as the relieving force approached.

Bensons defeat had a profound effect on Kitchener's self-confidence. Benson was his best commander advised by his best intelligence officer. Kitchener wrote "The Boers observe the movements of a column from a long way off, only showing very few men, and then having chosen some advantage, in this case the weather, they charge in with great boldness and the result is a serious casualty list. Benson's was one of the best columns....if a column like his operating 20 miles outside of our lines is not safe, it is a very serious matter and will require large additions to our forces to carry on the war...what makes me anxious is, if they can act in this way with Benson's column, how far easier it would be for them to catch some of my less efficient columns."

As the facts emerged, it transpired that Benson's rear-guard had fought heroically and had sacrificed themselves to protect the column, 66 men being killed and 165 wounded. The Boers had also suffered casualties including the death of the capable General Opperman. So the action was not clear cut. After a month or so in Pretoria, the regiment was sent out under Colonel Gore into the southern Transvaal to round up some scattered commandos. John was not with them as he had received orders to join General Bulfins column as his ADC, which was presumably a reflection of his experience in the field and recognition also of winning the V.C. The Regiment left camp at 3 a.m. on 12 December and John wrote "I said goodbye – I wonder when I shall see them again". It was not to be for a while. He took the very slow train ride to Bloemfontein and stayed at the Bloemfontein hotel ("bad"). There he met Curteis, an old groom who had joined the Scots Greys and borrowed a Cape cart to take his belongings to

Thabouchen, camping alone on the veldt and passing through Savana Port. He found Thabouchen "a rotten town - I put up at a hotel which was full of flies".

He joined a convoy at Thabouchen but decided to sleep late on their first day together as the countryside was clear of Boers; he caught up with them halfway to De Wetsdorp. He had dinner with officers from the Imperial Yeomanry and reached Bulfin on the following day, (20 December) finding to his chagrin that the staff mess was full up. His close colleagues were to be Dorrien Smith, as staff officer, Chambers as intelligence officer and Jackson. Dorrien Smith was commissioned a Second Lieutenant in the Rifle Brigade on 4 May 1898, and promoted to Lieutenant on 3 February 1900. On the outbreak of the Boer war, his Battalion was sent to South Africa, and he was mentioned in dispatches, and received the Distinguished Service Order (DSO) for his services during the war. He was promoted to Captain on 22 January 1902. On the death of his father in 1918, he succeeded as Lord Proprietor of the Isles of Scilly, a position he held until 1920 when the lease for the majority of the Isles of Scilly was handed back to the Duchy of Cornwall, Dorrien-Smith retaining control only over Tresco.

He is not to be confused (easy though that is!) with Smith Dorrien one of the few officers to escape the debacle of Islandlhwana in the Zulu war and then just by the skin of his teeth after spurring his horse from a high cliff into the Buffalo River with the Zulus close behind. Later he became renown as the General who held back the Germans at the battle of Le Cateau during the retreat from Mons in 1914, thereby saving the British Army from rout. He commanded a division in the Boer War. Sadly he was sacked soon after by the narcissistic and feeble General French after Le Cateau for not obeying orders….

The nearby villages were deserted and on 23 December, John rode out to Mafikeng "a nice little out of the way place" with Dorrien Smith. Several officers that he knew were recovering from enteric fever there and he received hospitality from Commissioner Kennan and his wife. The hero of Mafeking was of course Baden Powell who was a 5th Dragoon and has been at Sialkote. John also enjoyed talking to a French missionary whom he met on the road. He had a great Christmas which evidently became too jolly for one of his staff. On 26 December he wrote dryly; "I sacked Mitchell the man servant who developed a Christmas taste for old brandy and champers". On 27 December, he patrolled to Bloemfontein, some 20 miles away but made no contact. On 28 December, he went out foraging with another officer and some Africans but was evidently caught by farmers as he was "promptly chased into camp again". More serious business was afoot however as on his return, he discovered that a defence post had been attacked by Boers and a large number of horses and mules taken. John helped to recover all but eight horses and trekked on to Seville where the year and his diary end uneventfully.

In the final phase of the war the British strategy was to establish "protected areas" centred on Bloemfontein, Pretoria and the Rand and then work progressively outwards from these areas clearing them of guerrillas and restoring civilian life. The key to the system was the extension of the blockhouse lines which had been originally installed in January 1901 to protect the railways. By May 1902 there would be over 8,000 blockhouses covering 3,700 miles and guarded by at least 50,000 white troops and 16,000 African scouts. There were three main centres of Boer resistance; the north - east corner of the Orange River Colony (ORC) where De Steyn and De Wet had up to 2,500 men in the plains between Reitz, Lindley, Bethlehem and Basutoland; secondly, the semi-deserts of the Transvaal where De La Rey had 2,200 men beyond the Magaliesburg and thirdly the plains of the Eastern Transvaal where Botha had returned after Natal.

The aim within the cordon formed by the blockhouses (which were in sight of each other and connected by telephone), was to pursue and harry the guerrillas, bringing them to battle if possible but also provoking exhaustion, desertion and surrender. But the war of the columns was a confused and shapeless kind of war; catching the guerrillas proved difficult and sometimes the hunter became the hunted. The Army gradually learnt from its adversary, abandoning wagon trains and travelling light with only the supplies that could be carried by each horseman; marching at night and attacking the enemy's laager at dawn, firing rifles from the saddle, investing heavily in intelligence gathering , deploying effectively black scouts and guides.

The pendulum still swung however between the sides. In December following three successful raids by Colonel Rawlinson's column in the Transvaal, serving under Major General Bruce Hamilton's overall command, Botha's commandos were so crippled that Kitchener decided to transfer the columns to the Orange River Colony (the British renaming in 1900 of the Boer Orange Free State) in search of Steyn and De Wet. The latter was lying low in the triangle of Lindeley, Bethlehem and Reitz waiting for his chance. He chose Christmas day. The place was Tweefontein, the unsupported eastern end of a blockhouse line that was

134

being pushed from the railhead at Harrismith to link up with the line coming from Kroonstad. The defending forces were divided into four units and De Wet struck at the weakest, an Imperial Yeomanry detachment encamped at Groenkop. Once again the British failed to learn the lesson of Majuba; no pickets were stationed below the steepest face of the hill and the Boers struck hard after climbing it using a gully under a hazy moon. The result was heavy British casualties (expanded bullets were used by the Boers) and another British humiliation.

Kitchener had decided on assuming command after Roberts returned home to reorganise his forces. He created 38 Brigades out of the old divisions and deployed them in areas where the Boers were particularly active. The map was divided into squares, each covered by a group of brigades and each unit given a clear tasks and a well-defined area in which to act. Provision camps were established, effort placed on mounting more troops and lightening the columns. The next move was to improve the tactics by organising country wide sweeps with enormous care. Within a set area a number of columns would begin moving in a carefully coordinated manner. Each would march in a designated direction until they reached the boundary of their territory. They would then return to their starting point to surprise any Boers moving in behind them before setting off again in another direction. This complicated quadrille in which thousands of men moved around the empty veldt with clockwork precision was an extraordinary concept of war. It was wearing on man and beast and handicapped by the poor map- making standards of the day as well as the fleetness of the enemy.

Whatever the ultimate judgements on the value of the blockhouse system (and the debate still goes on) it appears that the use of super columns spread out across the veldt at an interval of one man every ten yards for 54 miles was beginning to grind down the Boers. Whilst De Wet and Steyn broke out through the wire in the Lindley area to escape the first sweep in February, a steady harvest of exhausted horses, cattle and demoralised fighters fell into the bag, notwithstanding poor co-ordination and a failure to create a proper line of command by Kitchener. Two innovations however placed additional strain on his enemy; firstly the use of Africans both as armed scouts and guides in the columns and blockhouses extended British strength (about 20,000 in total were deployed), secondly the reversal of the "concentration camp" policy left the care of families to the guerrillas, which added to their preoccupations at a critical phase. In the second sweep in February De Wet once again escaped but Meyer's commando of 800 men plus cattle and horses surrendered at Lang Riet. The third drive in March was a flop - De Wet and Steyn broke right out of the ORC and joined De La Rey in the Western Transvaal. Worse was to follow; De La Ray smashed a wagon convoy under Lieutenant Colonel Von Donop at Yzer Spruit on 24 February and then emboldened by success , knocked out a column of 1200 men at Tweebosch, capturing General Methuen in the process. Kitchener refused to emerge from his room for two days.

It turned out that once again, the Boers were unable to turn a tactical victory to strategic account. De La Rey was thrown back onto the defensive and two weeks later a six man delegation of Boers headed for Pretoria to talk about ending the war. On 11 April, the very day that the train carrying Botha, Smuts, De Wet, Steyn and the other leaders clanked into

Pretoria, the final significant engagement of the war was being fought out at Rooiwal, two hundred miles to the west. The frustrations of fighting in the Western Transvaal were exceptional. It was partly the terrain, a half wilderness of rolling sandy plains intersected by shallow river valleys, dry except in the rainy season and almost as desolate as the Karoo. De La Rey had perfected the principle that best ensures survival - invisibility. He emerged only to feed on convoys and had under his command 3000 veteran "bitter - enders" who had been as often as not opposed by the kind of callow half-trained Yeomanry serving under Methuen. Kitchener set his machine in motion and for the first time corrected a major strategic error by delegating command to all of the 13 columns in the field to Ian Hamilton.

De La Rey had cleared the territory of African families so the British were poorly served for intelligence. Their plan was simple - it was for three super - columns of around 2,000 men each to march southwards from the blockhouse line at Klerksdorp to the point where the Brakspruit and Little Hart's river flowed into the Great Hart's river. This fertile area had been De La Rey's main hunting ground. The Boers would expect the British to continue westward, but in fact they would then double back and squeeze the Boers against the blockhouse line as they attempted to escape south. After a muddle involving one of his column commanders, which fortuitously confused the Boers, dawn on the morning of 11 April found the British in a line of hastily dug trenches about 20 miles long from close to the Great Hart's river to east off Boschbush. The western part of the line at Rooiwal, which had been the weakest, was now the strongest containing 3,000 men under Kekewich's command. Hamilton knew from his intelligence that there were Boers ahead but action commenced before the drive could begin.

The Boers natural gift for tactical surprise had hitherto won them numerous victories in defence and attack. Moreover their ability to gallop and fight from the saddle firing their rifles in motion had been honed over the last months. But they had now overreached themselves. They needed not only courage, good luck and bad weather to succeed but also terrain that was pro - Boer. This was not the case at Rooival. There was no cover or camouflage for attackers, no trees, no kopjes, no kloofs. By contrast the stony hillside of Rooival hid Kekewich's men like a curtain. The Boers, led by Generals Kemp and Potgeiter galloped on to destruction as if at Balaclava. About a mile and a half from Rooival they breasted the final rise to confront disturbing odds; they numbered 1700 in all, without field guns and opposite them were over 3000 dismounted infantry, supported by eight guns.

In their attempt to out - do De La Rey's achievements they threw caution to the winds. They cantered on, forming a mass phalanx two, three and four deep. The guns began to tear holes in their line but they galloped ahead, expecting the British to turn and run which they had done before. There was some panic amongst the Yeomanry and the Boers were assisted by some poor shooting, but they shattered themselves on the line and Potgeiter reached 30 yards from the South African Constabulary before he was shot from his saddle. Around him lay 50 dead Boers and many wounded. The rest broke and fled. The British failed to follow up their victory with the dash that might be expected, but it was effectively all over.

The site of Rooival is a desolate spot on the veldt where the lack of cover even today makes Potgeiter's charge self-evidently suicidal. A simple marker indicates the site which seems unchanged from the time when a photograph was taken of Potgeiter's sprawled body and dead horse.

By 15 May, National Delegates elected by the Commandos scattered across the veldt had reached Vereeniging, 50 miles south of Pretoria. Each of the 60 delegates was asked to report on his own district. There were recognised to be three main obstacles to continuing the war; shortage of horses, shortage of food and the miserable conditions of the women and children who had remained with the commandos on the veldt. The Transvaal commandos were in a parlous state on all three counts, moreover, the retaliatory raid by the Zulu chief Sikobobo on the Boers at Holkranz only underlined the vulnerability of the families to native attack, a fear that had hitherto not been realised notwithstanding Boer treatment of the natives, including the massacre of the black civilian population at Modderfontein. In the Free State the situation was better and further resistance would have been possible

Smuts summed up the situation in the Cape as hopeless; the commandos could maintain themselves, but there would be no general uprising and the cause had to stand or fall by what happened in the Republics. The case for ending the war was essentially that it was ending anyway; the Volk were increasingly divided as many Boers rallied to the British side (by the end a fifth of the fighting Boers were with the British). The prospect facing the commandos was their gradual extrusion into the deserts and forests and the disintegration of the unity of the Volk. Finally, even De Wet recognised that the Free State could not struggle on without the Transvaal's help. After several weeks of tangled negotiation, on 31 May the delegates voted by 54 to 6 in favour of Kitchener's peace. A few days later, the trek to the ports began; all but 20,000 of the 250,000 British troops in South Africa were being sent home or their units disbanded.

Chapter 11

The Fifth Dragoons return to India

The Indian Government had been pressing for a very long time to have one of the four Cavalry regiments that it had lent for the Indian contingent to be sent back as their absence seriously affected the proportion between European and native troops in this particular arm. The senior regiment, the 5th Dragoons were chosen to return. From January to March they had been brigaded in Warm Springs, near Johannesburg with the Scots Greys who suffered losses from contact with a large force of Boers at Nigel's Mines on February 18, the situation being retrieved by successful rear-guard action from Squadrons B and D of the Dragoons. They saw action again from their Springs base in March before entraining for Durban on the 19th and from thence embarking on the SS Mohawk for India. They then proceeded to Lucknow where they were quartered until February 1904.

In the meantime, the war continued for John Norwood who before it came to a close, distinguished himself again whilst Staff Officer to Bulfin's column by being mentioned in Despatches. He ended the campaign with both the Queen's and King's South African Medals (bearing respectively 2 and 4 clasps to denote the actions in which he was engaged). For a period he was placed on duty with the 9th Lancers at Potchefstroom and it is not clear when he caught up again with his regiment but it is probable that he rejoined them in India at least by the time that peace was concluded in mid 1902. When in February 1904 however, they departed Lucknow for South Africa for another tour of duty, he was left behind presumably in preparation for his posting in December 1904 as Adjutant of the Calcutta Light Horse (CLH) and the Chota Nagpur Rifles where he was to stay for the next three years. Norwood's close friend, 2nd Lieutenant Panchaud who features frequently in his diary, belonged to the C L H and it was of course the custom for up and coming young officers to spend part of their early careers as staff officers to Indian Regiments.

The Chota Nagpur Regiment was raised in 1891 as the Chota Nagpur Mounted Rifles and formed part of the Cavalry Reserve in the British Indian Army. It was based on the great plateau to the west of Calcutta and was renamed the Chota Nagpur Light Cavalry in 1910 then the Chota Nagpur Regiment in 1917. The regiment was disbanded subsequent to India's independence in 1947. A light horse regiment was roughly equivalent to a battalion in strength (400 men) and its troops typically fought as mounted infantry rather than traditional cavalry.

When Kitchener became C- in-C in 1903 he was determined that the Indian Army should profit from the lessons painfully learnt from the Boers, the first enemy that the British had faced armed with high velocity rifles and quick firing artillery. The main lesson for the cavalry was that the horse's job was not "shock action" but to carry riflemen and machine gunners to the point where they could use their weapons to best effect. The Indian Army, like the British longed for the charge with lances and the new straight, thin bladed cavalry thrusting sword with no cutting edge, thirty years too late. Elandslagte had been the last hurrah of this kind of attack.

Each Indian Regiment had 12 officers per battalion and they were usually the cream of the Sandhurst cadets. The average officers spare time interests tended to be sporting rather than intellectual. He believed that strenuous exercise was necessary to health and sexual abstinence which was the lot of officers in India at the time. Cavalry officers were entitled to two horses but often spent money on more for polo, which together with shooting and pig sticking were the principal entertainments. No one overworked - the days routine ended at lunch which was followed by a long siesta and games and sports in the evenings.

The Calcutta Light Horse were "irregular" like nearly all Indian Cavalry regiments, a term defined by three characteristics; an attitude of mind, an emphasis on regimental differences and idiosyncrasies, a slight disdain for excessive enthusiasm and parade ground precision; a loose practical khaki uniform for service and for ceremonial occasions,  the most splendid of Indian style uniforms; the "Sirdar" system whereby each "Sowar" (Cavalryman) owned the horse that he rode and the equipment he wore. The quality of the men was at least as high as their British counterparts in cavalry and infantry skills; they were well trained and there was little or no crime. Every officer had to speak Urdu (English was never used) to a high standard as well as one of the village languages.

The "Sowar" looked upon even a subaltern as his mother and father, who would not only command him in battle and go in front to get shot first but would see that he was trained,

clothed, fed, paid and received preferential treatment from the civilian authorities in his village. Nothing was thought more important than to preserve that relationship. The Indian Officers were links between the British and their men, acting as advisors and examples of what could be achieved to the ranks and sorting out disciplinary problems informally. They expected high standards of soldierly qualities from the British officers and were treated in turn with great respect. As Adjutant, John Norwood would have been responsible for vetting Indian officer candidates with the advice of his Indian colleagues to guide him. There were no training depots; recruit training fell to the Adjutant and his Woordie Major.

We have no diaries to help us for John's Indian period but his attachment to the Indian Army must have proved memorable as there he met again Lilian Blanche Marie Collen, the daughter of Sir Edwin Henry Hayter Collen, Secretary to the Government of India Military Department, Shimla. As we have noted,

Collen was a considerable military figure who went on to serve in the Afghan war following adventures in Sudan and Abyssinia. The Indian Office Library contains numerous references to documents on military - Administrative matters written by Collen.

 Lilian and John were married at the Church of all Saints, Malabar Hill on 5 March 1904. Their first son, John was born on 15 July 1905 and baptised at Christchurch, Shimla on 19th September, by which time his father was a Captain. The couple lived at 2 Upper Wood Street Calcutta in an attractive property which is just across the road from what is now the Sanctuary Club, housed in a large neo colonial mansion. It seems that after his period in India, John re-joined his regiment in November 1907 in Bloemfontein in South Africa where they had been serving without major incident since 1904. In that same month, an advanced party under Major Clay, Captain Stott and Lieutenant Herapath left South Africa for Ballincollig, Ireland to form a depot for the 5th Dragoons. On December 2 1907 the Regiment sailed from Durban on the Braemar and arrived on December 29 in Southampton. It entrained the same day for Dublin and arrived there on the 30th where it was quartered in the Marlborough Barracks after having been on Foreign Service for more than 15 years. Only two officers had seen continuous service since that time - Colonel Kennard and Major Winwood.

By this time John's son was coming up to two years old and there are two very revealing letters from this period which are very whimsical and which showed John's love for his two year old son. The first was written from the Cavalry Club in Piccadilly on 20.02 1907. "My Dear Boy, I thank you for yours of no date. Please do not apologise for having written in pencil - you know that I am only too delighted to see your fist in any form, nor need you, my dear boy, have apologised for having written it with both hands at once - I regard it as surely proof of a most exceptional brain power- a power of which I saw distinct promise 18 months ago. Take care of your mother and Aunt Amy, make it your special care that the former does not fall overboard and do tell the steward to look after Aunt Amy well so that she does not get too thin, Your affectionate father, John". It appears that Lilian and Amy were off to France or Germany.

Later when John was by now in Dublin with the Regiment, he wrote a further letter; "Marlborough Barracks, Dublin. 1908 "My darling John, I am writing you a letter because you can read round O's and N's so well that you will soon be able to read letters. Give mother a kiss for me and with much love and kisses, you very loving father John"

John was not accompanied by his wife as far as we know when he was in Ireland and it would be interesting to know how the officers' families coped with the changes. It must be assumed that Lilian knew what to expect from her own family background but it could well be that John Norwood himself was becoming tired of the life by this time as within a year he had left the Army.

It is difficult to know whether John's departure had anything to do with the opportunities for promotion in peacetime or the boredom of garrison life in Ireland; a study of the Army List suggests that everyone moved upwards on a conveyor belt at the same stately pace. He had become a Captain in 1905 at the age of 29 and over the next 4 years reached 4th in seniority among the Captains in the 5th Dragoons (furthermore, JL Melvill the next in seniority had already transferred to the Pay Corps). It was not loss of prospects therefore that caused him to move on. The indications are that he was a restless soul and furthermore, had the private means to consider other interests. His Boer War Diary records that he had about £20,000 invested in shares in both the family firm of Wigan's and various South African mineral interests in 1901, so conceivably, the life of a gentleman of leisure called, giving him an opportunity to contemplate his future.

John resigned his commission in June 1909 and joined the sugar company Gartons in which he had made investments many years since. In 1882, the pioneering sugar refiner William Garton moved his premises from Canute Road in Southampton, where he had been based since 1847, to a new refinery at Southampton Wharf in Battersea. Originally a brewer, Garton had developed a type of invert-sugar, which he called "saccharum" that was ideally suited for the brewing industry, so he moved into producing that rather than beer and thereby made a fortune. The site as Battersea was known as the Garton, Hill and Company sugar refinery and it was a large employer in the area. It was eventually absorbed by Tate and Lyle and occupied a very large area indeed alongside the Thames.

John had not had much time in India to get to know his future in laws as Sir Edwin Collen had finished his career in Delhi in April 1901 and returned to the UK via Australia where he was delegated to represent India at the opening of the Australia Parliament. He then bought a house called The Cedars in the small Essex village of Kelvedon which had the advantage of being on a railway line to London. His final work for the Army was to serve as a member of the Regulations Committee of the War Office and as Chairman of the Staff College Committee. He was a founder member of the Royal Asian Society. He wrote and spoke frequently on Indian political and military affairs, his writing ranging from letters to the press to articles in the Encyclopedia Britannica and the specialized academic press. There is every indication that The Cedars was a haven for Lilian Norwood and the children as they came along, especially when John was posted to Ireland. The children enjoyed trips to the beach at Frinton on Sea which later commemorated John's life by naming a street after him, Norwood Road, which still exists.

A flavor of family life at The Cedars can be gleaned from an article written in the thirties by General Collen's nephew on the Rigby side of the family (Lady Collen's father was Charles Rigsby, builder of the Holyhead breakwater). The writer concerned was also called Charles Rigby and in "The House with Cypress Trees" he describes the Collen home. He notes that Lady Blanche had acquired a reputation as a brilliant hostess in India and the General received the thanks of both Houses of parliament on his retirement, but they were content to live a quiet country life. The house contained photographs of Lord Kitchener, Lord Roberts and the Curzons as well as personal friends. There were also miniatures by Henry Collen, the General's father and also paintings of the beautiful Frederica Remde, Lady Collen's mother by her father Frederiche Remde, the Hofmeister of the Grand Duke of Weimar. Collen used to sit in his study finishing a leader for the Times, or "middle" for the Saturday Review. His literary style was faultless, polished yet alive and he would receive occasional tickets from Lord Curzon to the Stranger's Gallery to keep up with debates. He also enjoyed excursions in his car with the family to Frinton on Sea.

Rigby says "It was Sir Edwin's simplicity and human kindness, rock like strength and severity, tempered surprisingly by an almost womanly tenderness that inspired respect. He had a reserve that precluded many intimate friendships but for those about him, he could never show enough solicitude.

One afternoon, returning from a country walk, we visited an old soldier who was bed ridden and horribly huddled up with rheumatoid arthritis. There were tears in Sir Edwin's eyes when we came out of the cottage. It was at such moments that one loved him. His silences were always more eloquent than his speeches." He died after an afternoon's tennis which was fatally strenuous for a man of nearly 70.

Rigby remembered the company assembled for the funeral at the Cedars. John Norwood was there. Rigby remembered because "I was young and John was over 6 feet tall, a story book hero come to life in his gorgeous Dragoon Guards uniform, with scarlet tunic, silver helmet with gaily flying plumes and clanging spurs and sword in the medieval church. As the solemn service proceeded, my eyes were riveted to John's fine, brown curly head. A year or two later, John himself had joined the goodly company in heaven".

On 10 April 1911 John gave away his sister Amy in marriage at St James Church Lancaster Gate to Ward Coldridge a barrister who

operated on the western circuit. Amy was 38 and living in Leinster Gardens at the time of her marriage. John and Amy had always been quite close as is clear from the tone of the journal that he dedicated to her concerning his Kashmir journey. This relationship was probably fostered by the early death of their parents leaving them to fend for themselves, as Amy was 4 years older than John; she presumably filled the gap left by the death of his mother. They lived together in Oakley Street Chelsea before he married. As she had independent means, it is likely that she did not pursue any kind of career; at least none is indicated in the record. As mentioned earlier Amy had been educated in Beckenham which was where she met Lillian Blanche Collen, John's future wife and introduced her to the family. The Browns of Hampstead into whose family the Norwoods had married possibly also played a nurturing role and for those reasons were recognised in Amy's Will.

Ward Coldridge had been married before to a lady slightly older then himself, Julia Helma Mott whom he married at St John the Evangelist in Notting Hill when he was 37 and she was 40. She died in the first quarter of 1910 leaving the modest sum of £670 which was only probated on Ward's own later death. He did not let the grass grow under his feet before marrying Amy and there is an intriguing entry in the shipping record which shows that in the autumn of 1910 they visited New York together, returning on the passenger liner Minnewaska. One imagines that honour was satisfied by separate cabins.

Ward was a man of modest origins who made good. He came from Devon and his father was a Commercial Traveller who did well enough to send his son to the Grammar School in Exeter and thence to Oxford. He studied at Lincoln's Inn and operated largely in the West of England until he took silk and became a

King's Counsellor in 1912. He specialised in chancery cases, relating to bankruptcy, gambling and copyright on which he wrote several learned tomes. Whilst he owned homes in various desirable areas of central London such as Holland Park and Ladbroke Grove, he also had a country place in Kensing near Sevenoaks, close to Norwood territory, called Pilgrim's Cottage. He was appointed one of the Registrars of Bankruptcy just three months before he died in 1926. They had no children.

Chapter 12

Outbreak of War

Great Britain at War with Germany" ran the headline of the Daily News and Leader on August 5 1914. "At 11.17 last night it was announced that a state of war existed between Great Britain and Germany. Great Britain delivered an ultimatum to Germany yesterday and demanded a reply by midnight. This action followed Germany's declaration of war on France and Belgium and the receipt of official news during the forenoon of the invasion of Belgian territory". The leading article went on to say that "Great Britain is prepared for war. The Navy is mobilised and at sea; the Army is being mobilised. Men and youths are flocking to the colours and crowds besiege the recruiting offices".

It is difficult to imagine in the light of what we know about John's character that he would have been other than stirred by this momentous event and would have wanted to be part of it. Predictably he re-joined the 5th Dragoons in August 1914 and as the regiment like the rest of the Army was very much under strength, found his services welcome. Like other reservists keen to get to France, he presumably passed Colonel Ansell's simple examination - essentially, as long as a man was a first class shot, his age was not considered. Jumps were erected in the riding school at the South Cavalry

(Beaumont) Barracks and those who could get around the course bare - backed were accepted. In fact, Ansell was so keen to have him that he sent a grey Rolls-Royce to collect him.

John took out life insurance in London before departing on Friday 13th for £10,000 - "war risk was £7.7.0 extra!" It is doubtful that this kind of insurance would be available for much longer - and the date was ominous. He then wrote a farewell letter to the children; "August 14. Chumleigh Farnham. 1914. My Darling John Robin and Di, just a few lines to say goodbye and wish you all a very peaceful and happy time. Mummy will be home before this letter gets to you. I have asked her to buy you all a present from me. I have your photos in a case, Ever your loving father, John"

The Regiment sailed for France on the SS Cestrian, a transatlantic passenger ship, on Sunday 16 August, consisting of a total strength of 549 all ranks; John Norwood was in B Squadron commanded by Major Head. The 5th formed part of the 1 st Brigade of the Cavalry Division. The Cestrian later became a casualty of war on June 24th, 1917, on a voyage from Salonica to Alexandria with 800 troops and horses; it was sunk by the German submarine UB-42, 4 miles SE of Skyros Island in the Aegean (the burial site of the poet Rupert Brooke). Only 3 crew members were killed due to the discipline among the embarked troops who took successfully to the boats.

John wrote in his diary "Saturday 14. We paraded 6.00 a.m. We entrained at Farnborough. We left at 8.30 a.m. for Southampton, arriving there about 11 am – it was pouring with rain – I got some food from Lady Lois Danes - a great boon. In rest camp amidst mud and rain for some hours- thence to quay- we embarked in the Cestrian, finished by midnight. Sunday 14. The boat at left at dawn steering an extraordinary course to avoid mines. We arrived (France) at about 3 pm. Arthur Dick was on board, very gorgeous in red tabs. (Note; this is Colonel Sir Arthur Robert Dick, K.B.E., C.B., C.V.O., Inspecting Officer, Frontier Corps, Indian Army) We reached a huge hanger on the quay about 11 p.m. This shed was so big that a cavalry brigade and a half with horses and an infantry battalion plus 2000 large barrels of beer and endless stacks of supplies only part filled it."

"Monday 15. We lunched in town after a parade at 7 a.m. - 2 p.m. through Harfleur- apparently the French are much touched by our coming. We are all too solemnly stopping to shake hands. I had my hair cut by a most amusing barber – too short for Lil's taste. I dined off bully in the hanger; we paraded at midnight and entrained. The train left on Tuesday 17th at 6 a.m. We are under sealed orders. We got there at 11 p.m. rested in a field for the night, paraded at 6 a.m. and marched on." In the evening of 17 August 1914, the Regiment entrained again and arrived at Hautmont on the 18th, marching into billets at Colleret. On the 21st the 5th moved into Villers-Saint-Ghislain with the Cavalry Division. "Wednesday 18. I am writing this in an empty French chateau – or rather a big farm which, with a walled garden, huge barns and stables, marbled floors and polished wood floors, just fills the eye." By this stage, John and the 5th are on the outskirts of Mons.

"I have felt sometimes that I tried you too much in coming; but I am so proud to be here, so very much more proud to think you let me come, that I would not have it otherwise. All my love, John" This is probably the most poignant of John's letters which adds to a note in his diary dated 1 August in which he says "Germany and Austria declare war. Lil like a true dear wife agrees, without my suggesting, it to my re-joining the 5th." There

Retreat from Mons

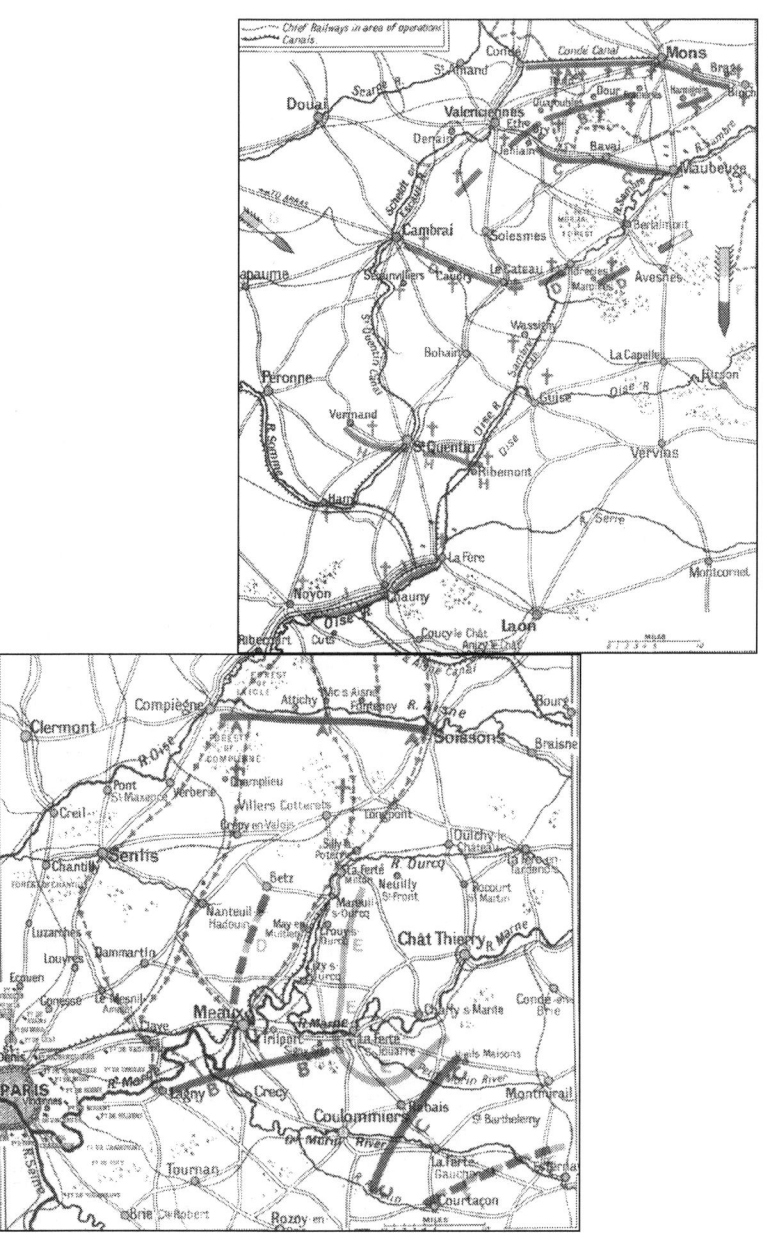

must have been many times during her many years of widowhood that Lilian regretted her generous assent to this position. Contact with the Germans occurred on 22 August along the River Haine but only in the form of distant shell bursts. On Sunday 23 August, firing to the north signaled the opening shots of the battle of Mons. Namur in Belgium fell on this day and the 5th French Army began falling back on the line Givet-Philippeville-Maubeuge General French decided to retreat also on the line Maubeuge- Jerlain.

The Regiment found itself on the extreme left of the British line at Mons with a gap to its right through which the Germans attacked on August 24 from Thulin. The Regiment retired and was then ordered with other elements of the Ist Cavalry Brigade to cover the exposed flank of the infantry as the BEF began its long retreat to the Marne. The 5th Dragoons continued to provide the rear-guard to the Division for several days, slowing the enemy with gunfire and supporting defensive artillery actions. No supplies got through so the 5th depended on iron rations. The roads were frequently clogged with a tangle of cavalry, infantry, guns and wagons. German shells occasionally fell quite close but to little effect, the men slept as best they could on the side of the road next to their horses.

The role that the Regiment was playing at this time was their classic responsibility - time after time extricating slower moving infantry and guns, and engaging in rear- guard actions to check the enemy. If this role had not been successfully discharged, General French would have been required to stand his ground and fight a daily battle. For example in the village of Solesmes, the infantry and artillery were in great danger of being cut off, so Captain Partridge deployed two dismounted troops of C

Squadron on the northern and eastern approaches to the village, holding up the German advance on the Valenciennes road for a considerable time and then executing a stepped withdrawal by deploying the rest of the Squadron to provide covering fire, losing not a single man, notwithstanding pretty continuous shelling. John Norwood's Squadron became separated at this time from the others as the retreat continued.

The Regiment participated in the holding action at Le Cateau with the Cavalry Division who were lightly engaged but helped to form rear and flank guard for the 4th Division. On 27 August after desultory fighting around Ronssoy, the regiment became detached from the rest of the 1st Cavalry Brigade in the dark and formed a unit with a stray squadron of 5th Lancers and another from the 11th Hussars under Colonel Ansell. On August 25 the German 2 Army made repeated efforts to break through the British Cavalry screen but failed, General Smith Dorrien's column crossed the Somme practically unmolested. Ansel's detachment held up a force of 4,000 German Infantry in the Villecourt area then fell back across the Somme reaching Nesle.

After passing through Nesle and crossing the Aisne, where the men were able to bathe in the river for the first time in many days, contact was re-established with the 1st Brigade at Compiegne on August 31. Ansell's detachment was broken up and the Regiment reformed with the re engagement of John Norwood's troop from B squadron who had been cut off with his men and accompanying signallers after the action at Solesmes on August 25th. The regiment billeted at Nery where a significant action took place.

The context for this fight was that Von Kluck believed that the

British had retreated in a south easterly direction and was intent on making use of the victory of the German 2nd Army over the French 5th Army to cut off their retreat to the south of Laon. He regarded the British Army as effectively having ceased to exist as a fighting force but was using his three Cavalry Divisions to protect his flank. In fact the British had retreated in a southerly direction opening a gap between their 5 and 4 Divisions as a consequence of the terrain over which they were retreating. Unknowingly therefore, the Germans advanced into this gap, ignorant of their adversary. The British First Cavalry Brigade was practically the only force in that gap.

Nery is a village that runs north - south and the 5th had the northern end (that nearest to the German line of pursuit) with their horses in the open. The morning of September 1 broke cool and misty - fog was so thick that it was impossible at first to see more than 20 yards. A few moments before 5 o'clock, an 11th Hussars patrol reported that it had bumped into a body of German cavalry who had chased it back to Nery. The 11th Hussars were in the middle of the town; the Bays held the south end and beyond them was a battery of Horse Artillery in the open. In the thick morning fog, proceedings unexpectedly opened with a burst of German shells over the village which sent everyone running for their lines to saddle up.

The first burst of fire wiped out L battery of the RHA, both gun and limber teams, and stampeded the horses of the detached Squadron of Bays. The 11th Hussars hardly suffered at all and the 5th Dragoons, slightly protected from view by the angle of the village, managed to stop their horses stampeding. A line of fire was built up on the eastern side of the village, three machine guns were brought to bear on the German guns which could just be seen through the mist and the gunners brought three big guns into position. Two of these were quickly destroyed but the third kept firing with machine gun accompaniment.

A and B Squadrons were quickly collected by Colonel Ansell and galloped north out of the village to turn the German right flank, leaving C Squadron to hold the north east corner. This daring manoeuvre deceived the Germans as to the strength of the force confronting them.

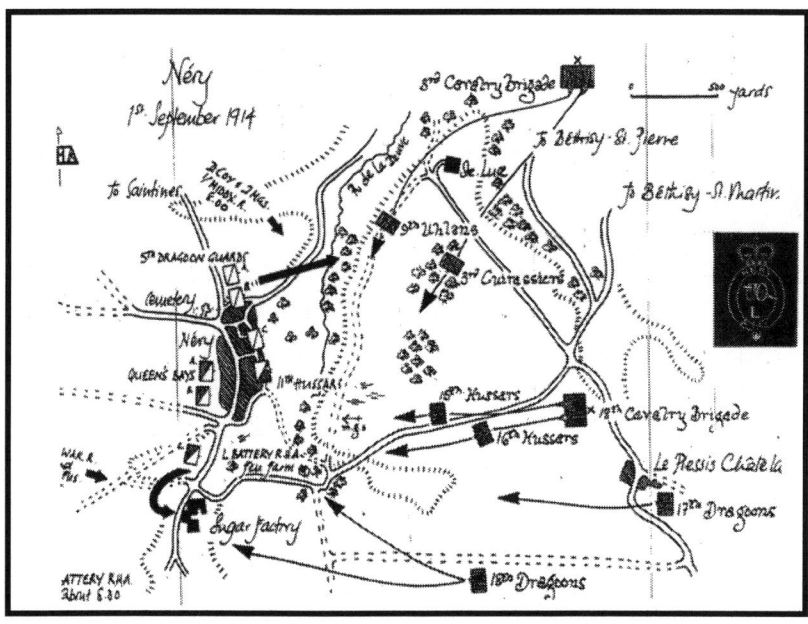

Consequently, they deferred pressing the attack until the arrival of reinforcements. However German artillery firing at 700 yards did great damage to the Bays and the RHA. Ansell's move had the desired effect however of forcing the Germans withdrawal and there is no doubt that the boldness with which the 5th charged home was the deciding factor of the day. But Ansell was killed together with ten others and about 20 were wounded. Corporal Peach and Sergeant Longford won the DCM for their actions, the latter for shooting ten Germans with rifle fire from a dismounted position. The Brigade was supported towards the end of the action by elements of the 19th Infantry Brigade and part of the 4th Division. Overall British casualties were 45 killed and 87 wounded. The Germans left 8 guns on the field, at least 30 dead and 78 prisoners.

As the Regimental Diary records; "It transpired that the Germans, who consisted of about a Cavalry Division with 10 or 12 guns, had blundered on to us in the fog. A wireless message from Von Der Marwitz, 4th Division Commander, was intercepted to the effect that this division was unable to fulfil its mission, as it had been heavily attacked by the English. The only desire of the English at Nery at that moment was to get outside an excellent breakfast!" The German losses were about the same as the British, they also lost their guns, but more importantly, they were discouraged from pressing down on the retreating column. The losses in horses could not have been less than 400, killed and stampeded.

Indirectly, the battle of Nery had very far reaching results. Von Kluck spent the whole of September 2 concentrating his forces and therefore lost whatever prospect he may have had of falling on the left flank of the French 5th Army. From now until September 5, the paths of the two Armies diverged.

The 5th continued their retreat towards Paris, passing through Borest and Ermenonville before spending a pleasant night in the orchard of the chateau at Moussy - le

- Vieux. John wrote to Lilian, confused about the date…..
"Either 23 or 20 August….. Dearest, I find that my dates were wrong in my last letter because the Monday Bank holiday ought to have been August 3rd. Thursday 19 we stopped in our French Chateau Wednesday and Thursday night and left on Friday, getting to a village some way off where we pitched in an orchard. We got into a large force of Germans at once and had to hold a strongish line of outposts. That night Friday we dug ourselves in, fortifying barns etc., however nothing came of it. They made a feeble attack on the right of where I was, but the 4th Dragoons scuppered a few of them in a charge and they fled, so all was well.

On Saturday night we marched at 7 and got here at 2 a.m. - we had a slack day waiting about saddled up but as I had been up till midnight on Friday, I got up at 2.30 yesterday and was glad to get bedded down in a barn here at 3 a.m. this morning. There is a battle going on about 3 miles away and as I write we are saddled up ready for a huroosh somewhere, so I write in haste. It is now 5 pm and I fear another night march."

"I am awfully fit and getting hard- the food is scrappy, apples, chocolate and laager at odd intervals. I have been playing with three little French kids on the village green - they were most excited over your photos. Last night we came through endless towns - just like the outskirts, say, of a Lancashire town and from 7 to 10 we were just shrieked at, with " Vive les anglais" by thousands and thousands - a most extraordinary sight and one I shall never forget. We know but little of how the war goes on and I would like so much to tell you all about it but I can't write names at all even though this letter is not of course going for weeks yet. Kisses from me to you, John"

"September 4. 1914, Dearest, A rest day today, the first we have had and it is much wanted for we have been very short of sleep, have seldom had our baggage and only had a shave about every three days. There is a good deal of food of sorts knocking about, bread apples and wine is our chief diet but I know nothing about where we go now and if I did , could not tell you. I do not think that anyone knows. I was so thankful to get your letter of August 15-19 and to hear how you are getting on. I am sure that with you and those three little souls in a row by the high bed, God will do what he sees fit and I am thankful and glad to hear of it."

"I am sorry for the Knight's German cousin, as you know I have a very fond spot for the Germans who I regard as our natural allies and I dislike the French - more since I have known them than before. But I must say that the way the Germans have burned whole districts and turned out the women has made me quite sick. I have stayed time after time in just perfect little country villages with good hospitable souls (the peasant French are most attractive) and before the day is over, have seen the whole valley and plain burning for miles. The Uhlans are dirty swabs, just marauders of bad stamp, but they are not much good as a fighter which I confess surprises me very much."

"Two days ago at Nery at dawn, 6000 of them with 2 batteries caught us on the hop, a hoary white fog had enabled them to surround us, but in half an hour we had got ten of their guns, although of course they gave us a hotting whilst we saddled up. There is no question which way this war is going only it may take some time – I do hope not too long."

"09.40 a.m. I just got mail but no further letters from you, only a postcard from John to whom I am writing, a postcard from you and some letters from various people of no interest. Everyone is very kind – please thank Mrs K for her PVC. Now on to your

163

letter- no one has my power of attorney, I will send you one when I can but it is really of no importance. I have written to Mr Cole re income tax. Please send me occasionally a box of Cohens (Piccadilly), No 3 Royal Beauties cigarettes. Also occasionally a pair of my own old socks- they are more comfortable.....Also my canvass boots - one in each packet marked "Boots Urgent". Also a pair of Stokwasser's stocking knitted putties – their shop is in Conduit Street. Fond loving thoughts dear heart, to you and yours, John."

The Marne was reached at Gournay where the regiment stayed for two days - almost in the suburbs of Paris but with no opportunity to enjoy its delights.On September 5 after crossing the Marne, the Regiment moved on to Luigny which was the limit of its retirement. The following day found them at Jouy-le-Chatel, preparing to advance North East against the flank exposed by the Germans as they manoeuvred to strike against the left of the French.

John's last letter to his wife was written on September 6. 1914. "5.30 a.m. Dearest, We got into this place last evening (Gournay) about 8 miles east of Paris and I sent you a wire hoping you might get it all right as they have taken off censorship at any rate, on this side. I cannot tell you all in detail, but having landed in Le Havre on the 16th we detrained at Busigny and went up to Belgium, getting up near to Tirlemont. From about Sunday 23rd till two days ago, we had usually to fight fairly hard. I think that the Germans are fine soldiers. Very slow and very methodical- they almost ring a breakfast gong in the middle of battle - the whole thing is method. Their guns are the devil – they had such legions of them - in fact masses and numbers seem to be the ruling factor. Fighting numbers like this with only our little push of about 3000 cavalry means disaster if one makes a mistake or misjudges things so at intervals, we have all had rather a twisting, although I am sure that the German losses have been far in excess of ours. We have done a strategic retirement on Paris and what the next move is, I do not know. We have lost a goodish few folk but….we are all fit and well."

"It sounds conceited but I am pretty well convinced from what I saw around Mons, Valenciennes, Arty, Le Cateau, Bohain, Angr, Dour, St Quentin, Noyon, Le Fert, Nery and Compiegne that given an equality of numbers, we should knock out Germany and that Germany would knock out France. I think that the French in everything but their front line troops are rotten and I still feel that our true allies should be the Germans. My dislike of the Frenchman has increased. I have had to shoot one of my horses."

"Dearest, I simply adored your dear letter and the eye picture of the family prayers. It was too much for me altogether. I am so glad and thankful. Ever dearest, your loving and devoted John."

.

Chapter 13

The Crossing of the Marne

On Monday 7 September, Sir John French issued his order of the day to the effect that the British had had a very trying time during the retirement but had performed well; it was now going to attack the Germans with the French all along the line. It was now the Germans return to retire and the allies to pursue….the great counter offensive had begun. On 7 September there was a head to head mounted charge at Fretox between the 9th Lancers and German Dragoons but the end of this type of warfare was signalled on the same day at Faujus when a German mounted Squadron was annihilated by dismounted Cavalrymen.

The Dragoons pressed on as the rear regiment of the 1st Brigade through Chevry and Choissy. At 2.30 am. On September 8th, the Regiment moved out as the vanguard of the brigade, with the responsibility of covering the advance of the 1st Army Corps. The first advance was through La Ferte-Gaucher and on to Launoy before descending into the valley of the Petit Morin. The three squadrons were strung out in line of advance as they approached the village of Sablonnieres. It was John Norwood's 38th birthday and he had just been given charge

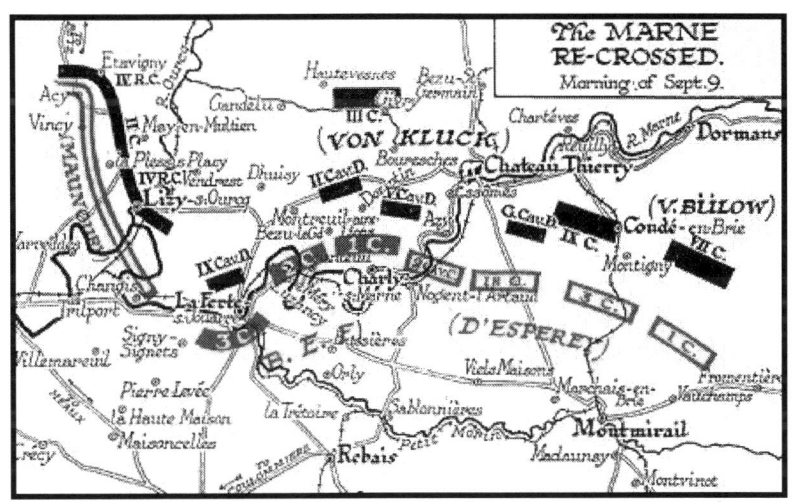

The MARNE
RE-CROSSED.
Morning of Sept. 9.

of Company B. The official Regimental Diary of the war records the action as the regiment moved down through woods towards the river.

"Captain Norwood reported Sablonnieres to be lightly held. Lieutenant Williams was left with one troop on the road in front of the village and could get no further owing to rifle fire. Captain Partridge, with two Troops of C, and Captain Norwood with three troops of B, went round by Bellot under orders to cross the river there - Bellot being in the hands of the French - and attack Sablonnieres from the East. A squadron was ordered to attack from the south on the left of Williams' troop.

Captain Partridge asked for assistance from the French who were held at the bridge at Bellot but was unable to obtain it. He deemed it impracticable to make so wide a turning movement as the passage of the river would entail, and therefore approached Sablonnieres by the main road from

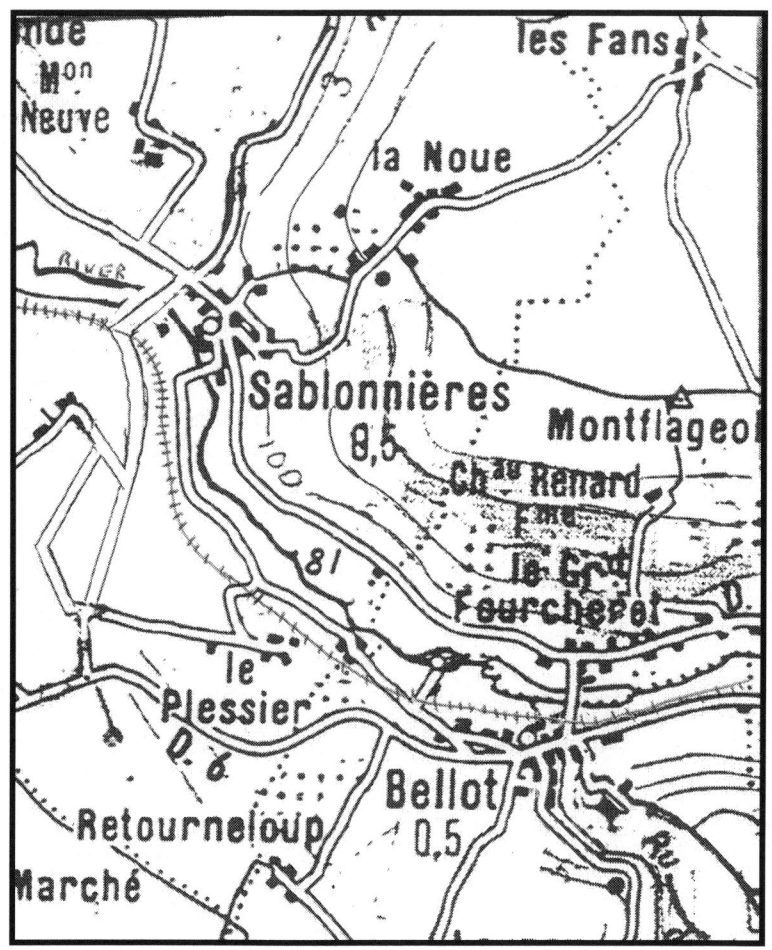

Bellot, on the south side of the river. He came into action about half - mile from the village in an open water meadow, where there was little or no cover, but it was the only position available as the river was unfordable. His attack was brought to a standstill by German rifle fire from the village and wood, and from trenches in rising ground just north of the river. Here both Captain Partridge and Captain Norwood were killed...Privates Wisdom and Fishlock were killed and

Sergeants Gough, Nunn and Coole wounded."

We know from a map in the Marie at Sablonnieres exactly where the incident took place as it shows the burial place of the horses which the villagers later interred where they fell. It is due west of the 100 metre contour line on the map where the road, river and railway are close together.

When the 11th Hussars arrived at Sablonnieres to assist the 5th Dragoons, Colonel Pitman of the Hussars, told the 5th to hold in their position on the low ground whilst he moved the 11th to higher ground. Two dismounted Squadrons began to work around the village to the west supported by elements of 2nd Cavalry Brigade. The German position however was very strong, the river was unfordable, the bridges barricaded and the approaches swept by machine gun fire. The gunners found it difficult to bring fire to bear on the village. In consequence all the morning was taken up forcing a crossing and it was not until the Ist Black Watch and the Ist Cameron Highlanders crossed the river at Bellot to threaten the Germans from the east flank that they gave way. As they ran through the meadows on the other side of the river, the dismounted Hussars approaching the village down the road through the centre of the village had their chance and opened fire causing great execution, raking also the hill on the north side of the river. The German Guard Cavalry Division soon resumed their retreat at a cost of about 60 casualties. The Hussars pushed on and struck north east, at first suffering friendly fire which was quenched by a heavy thunderstorm.

The 5th Dragoons crossed the Petit Morin, passed through passed through Sablonnieres and bivouacked that night at Replonges before pressing on towards the crossing of the

Aisne and the battle for the Chemin des Dames. Captain LR Lumley MP, and afterwards Lord Scarborough wrote in his book "The 11th Hussars" that "The day's fighting had been important. The line of the Petit Morin, which was strong and gallantly defended, and which the enemy intended to hold, had been forced. The French Armies on either side of the British had been brought to a standstill. In fact the Sixth French Army was in danger of being overwhelmed by von Kluck's desperate efforts to get out of the situation in which he had placed himself. The issue of the great battle was hanging in the balance and at French HQ all eyes were turned to the British Army to see if it could advance far enough to turn the scale. By breaking through the line of the Petit Morin on this day and by the advance made on the following day, the British effort was the deciding factor in compelling the Germans to retreat."

As a footnote to this history, according to the diary of the Second Battalion of the Welch Regiment, my father, Private William Murphy marched through Sablonnieres within hours of the death of John Norwood en route to the fight for control of the Chemin de Dames and later on to other battles in the Ypres salient. His son was to marry John's granddaughter 55 years later.

It is not difficult to recapture today the circumstances of the fateful action at Sablonnieres. The terrain is virtually unchanged as the front line quickly passed way beyond the village which was not therefore torn up by war. The Petit Morin flows sluggishly westward through a broad bottomed valley to its junction with the Aisne. The road from Rebais drops down to the river, crosses over it by an ancient bridge and climbs up the steep wooded scarp slope on the other side for a hundred feet or so before levelling out. The track of the old railway line that runs along the valley between Bellot and Sablonnieres is clearly discernible and the ruin of the railway station at Bellot stands mutely beside the line of the permanent way. Crossing the river at Bellot would not have been easy as it was also overlooked by the wooded escarpment and the flood plain of the river is broad there too. It is impossible to avoid a feeling of acute vulnerability when walking along the old line and following the route taken by the two squadrons. The deep shadows under the not so distant trees across the river seem desperately close and the imagined sound of heavy machine gun fire drifts coldly across the years.

It is clear from the official history of the 5th Dragoons that was written after the war on the basis of the Regimental diaries, that the action at Sablonnieres raises questions. "It would be very interesting to know what information Captain Partridge, who, as senior officer present, was in command of the force, got from the French at Bellot to cause him to modify the plan of attack. To the east of Sablonnieres, on the north side of the river, the ground is very steep, and covered with thick woods. There seems reason to believe that he learned that the Germans had strongly entrenched positions there, covering their left flank and that the best way of carrying out the spirit of his instructions was to attack along the railway on the south side of the river so as to enfilade their positions. Unfortunately, in doing so he came under severe fire from the village and wood immediately north of the river."

It seems that John Norwood was not hit in the opening fire but was killed trying to get help for some of the wounded, which would have been in character. We have a deposition written on

29 October before a Commissioner of Oaths by an NCO called Bertram Nunn, a Sergeant in the 5th for the details of his final moments.

"I knew and was well acquainted with the late John Norwood, a Captain in the 5th Dragoon Guards and a holder of the Victoria Cross, I having served with him in the Boer War. On the 8th of September 1914 I was present with the said John Norwood at the Battle of the Marne; France near the village of Sablonnieres in the District of Rebas and during the engagement with the enemy, the deceased had his horse shot under him. At this time, the Regiment was just beginning to retire from their position and this deponent (Nunn) was wounded, when the said John Norwood ran to me and assisted as far as possible and then started running to obtain the aid of one of the Medical Corps to attend to me, when I saw the said John Norwood shot dead, a bullet having gone through his neck and killed him. I saw the body of the deceased put into a cart and taken away to be buried and afterwards learned from Sergeant Hadida of the 5th Dragoon Guards that he had buried him in a suitable place."

Nunn had joined the Dragoons in 1900, served in South Africa and fought throughout the Great War notwithstanding his wounding in 1914. He married in 1917 the charmingly named Gertrude Scattergood and died in 1933 aged 54. He and Hadida (born 1881) were more than close friends - they married sisters and were witnesses at each other's wedding. Hadida had a Sephardic Jewish background, although born in the UK, and married Ethel Scattergood in 1916; he survived the war and died in 1943.

John and his comrades as well as others killed in the final assault, were eventually brought to Sablonnieres Communal

Cemetery. This is in the bend of the road before it drops down to a bridge across the river, a few steps away from the now abandoned railway crossing and the old ruined station which has a peeling sign on its facade and which has been converted into a traditional dwelling.

Scene of the Action - Sablonnieres, September 1914

In a letter written by Major Winwood, (later to rise to Lieutenant Colonel) commanding the 5th to Lilian Norwood dated September 11th, Winwood who was a good friend of John wrote; " Dear Mrs Norwood, we cannot say how sorry we all feel for you in your great loss. Dear old John was as usual leading his men on, attacking a bridge held by the Germans when he was shot. I am unable to let you know the name of the place where it happened, but when the censorship is over, I will let you know. An English clergyman who is attached to the Cavalry Division buried him with Captain Partridge and two other poor fellows in the cemetery and we have marked the spot. We will send you all his personal effects as soon as we can safely send them to base without fear of being lost en route. Our deepest sympathies are with you." (John's personal effects, hairbrushes etc, are with the family still).

A record of the memories recollected rather late in life of Major HEE Pankhurst MC who was second in command to Partridge with C Squadron fails to shine much light on the incident. He says "John Norwood and RC Partridge went off on their own to stalk and kill Germans with a couple of rifles. I was left in charge of the Squadron on a reverse slope. After they had been at it for a short while, Partridge was shot by a German sniper through the heart. Norwood stayed on for a bit, got fed up and started to walk back, and he was immediately shot. I thought that it was a poor thing to leave their men and go off like that. As they were Protestants, the local cure forbade burial within the Catholic cemetery nearby, and we had to bring them outside of the walls. I hope that they were eventually re-interred in one of the military cemeteries after the war".

There is scarcely an element of this account which squares with the two Regimental records or war diaries for that day, Nunn's testimony, or the conclusions to be drawn from the records at the Mairie. Far from two officers going off to have some fun shooting, the operation involved five troops and is best characterized as a reconnaissance in force. As France is a secular state the cure does not rule on use of the cemetery where they are all in fact buried. Perhaps we should generously attribute the inaccuracy of these remarks to the frailty of memory after the passage of time. Pankhurst had been with the 6th Royal Fusiliers and the Norfolk Regiment in 1900. He was in South Africa and transferred from the Mounted Infantry to the 5th in 1902 in the Boer War as there was a shortage of regular officers. He went

174

with them to Lucknow and back again to South Africa. He left the Dragoons in 1922. From various remarks that he made on his experiences, and his fellow officers, he made have considered himself a victim of snobbery in the Regiment which colored his attitude.

In addition to the usual telegram from the War Office informing Lilian of John's death, addressed to her at the family home at The Chestnuts, Hayward Heath, there was another telegram from the Private Secretary of King George sent from Buckingham Palace. This said "The King and Queen deeply regret the loss that you and the Army have sustained by the death of your husband in the service of his country. Their Majesties truly sympathize with you in your loss"

There was a heartfelt letter published in the Regiment magazine on 24 October 1914 under the title "Ex trooper's Tribute to Captain John Norwood VC, 5th Dragoon Guards under the name E Charles whom I have not been able to identify definitively.

"The letters "V.C" after Captain Norwood's name are sufficient to attest his qualities as a soldier; he was, as well as soldier, a man in the best sense of the word and there have been few officers in the 5th Dragoon Guards who have won the respect and liking of their men to a greater extent than in his case. His VC was won in the South African campaign when under fire he saved the life of one of the men of the Regiment. After the war, both in India and Africa "B" Squadron found in him a good officer in every way, and the personal interest that he took in his men was a thing that is all too rarely seen in the Service. Norwood knew his Squadron just as well as the Sergeant Major knew it, and that is saying a good deal. And the men knew him – they knew themselves well off in possessing him as a Squadron officer.

But it was not alone in connection with service with the colours that Captain John Norwood V.C. was a man of exceptional qualities. Owing almost solely to his efforts, the old Comrades association of the 5th Dragoon Guards was reorganized and put on a working footing. I do not remember exactly when Captain Norwood left the Colours, but I think that it must have been somewhere in 1908. In that year and in 1909, acting from the HQ of the OCA down in the Clapham Road, Captain Norwood was ready with advice and help for all the old soldiers of the Regiment who cared to come to him. He found a factory in the North of England which was willing to give employment and chances of promotion to capable men, and he sent dozens of men up to work there, men who but for him and his efforts, would have been among the unemployed and probably tramping the streets.

He found other situations for other men and did his best to help ex-soldiers of his old Regiment to keep their self-respect and attain to a position in the world. Not that he himself was a leisured man, able to give himself up to such an enterprise, for he occupied at that time, a position on the directing board of a large manufacturing firm and had all his energies occupied with productive work – except for such time as he gave the OCA.

There are instances within my knowledge of unostentatious charities that he was responsible for, incidents that stamp him as a good man. This is a term that a soldier uses rarely and from that fact, let its significance be judged. I know that after the war when men of my old Regiment are coming back to civilian life, there will be many a one who would be better fitted to face work and living if Captain Norwood were there to help him, for

Captain Norwood knew how to judge and place men – he was a psychologist as well as a soldier, as discerning as he was big hearted.

I count it as a privilege that I knew him better than did most of the rank and file of the Regiment, even better than the men of his own squadron. I feel, as many more must feel, that in reading the brief official mention of his name in the list that is watched and read more closely than any other part of the papers, I have been robbed of a friend – that there were many others whom the world and the Army and the 5th Dragoon Guards could have better spared. Yet I feel too, that he died as he would have wished, as a soldier and a British gentleman should. All honor to the memory of a brave soldier and a good man"

John clearly was also held in high regard by the employees of Gartons, whose views were quoted in a published obituary as follows, not differing much in tone and content than the previous remarks; entitled "Captain Norwood Killed in Action. Battersea Employees Grief."

"The late Captain Norwood was a partner in the firm of Garton and Sons. News of his death has occasioned the keenest grief amongst the hundreds of employees of the firm. Captain Norwood's popularity with them rivalled that of Sir Richard Garton himself and was heightened by their admiration of his fine qualities as a soldier. A hero in every sense of the word, Captain Norwood was especially a hero to those who knew him best. During the lamentable strike at the works in October last year, the men would do anything for Captain Norwood. He was at the head of those who stayed at their posts. Day after day, while the strike lasted, he remained with the men, working with the barrow and shovel harder than anyone and keeping everybody cheerful."

The obituary went on to repeat in conventional terms his record in winning the V.C. in South Africa etc. The cynical will no doubt conclude that the text very much reflects proprietorial attitudes at Gartons, however, it is not unlikely that John cast a rather dashing figure to the employees. There is plenty of evidence that he was a kindly man who had a sense of <u>noblesse oblige</u> in his dealing with his men and his employees. This old fashioned virtue, based on class, would be look at with askance in today's world. But it is worth remembering that in the Cavalry it had always been the tradition to put the officers last, after the horses and the men. The evidence suggests that he was loyal to family and friends but undoubtedly a warrior, exulting in action.

Chapter 14

Aftermath

The French have raised a traditional memorial to the dead of both World Wars at the entry to the village. It consists of the familiar figure of a poilu from the First World War standing at attention and gazing sternly over his grounded rifle. On the face of the plinth is inscribed "1914 - 1918 to the glorious memory of the men of Sablonnieres who died for France and to our valiant allies who fell in combat in Sablonnieres on 8 September 1914". On the rear of the plinth was carved the following "British soldiers fallen in combat - Captain Dalglisch, Captain Partridge, Captain Vowood, Lieutenant Wilson, Soldiers Uisdon, Fislock, Fostu and 13 unknown." It was clear that the mason had not been given the proper names of those who died and some of the confusion

may have been due to the circumstances of their death.

Next to the medieval church in the centre of the village is the Mairie which contains the records of what appears to be the transfer in July 1915 of the casualties of 8 September, both German and British, to the communal cemetery for reburial from their original resting place. Some of the names are misspelled and are only recorded correctly in the Commonwealth War Graves Commission book of Remembrance held at the cemetery. It is clear from that book that all 19 of those killed in the action are indeed known; most are from the Black Watch including "Dalglish" and Wilson. Foster was a 19th Hussar and Partridge, Norwood and Privates Wisdom and Fishlock belonged to the 5th Dragoons (Partridge was younger than Norwood but he had enjoyed a longer period of continuous service and was therefore regarded as the senior of the two and first appears in the Regimental list in 1902). The records at the Mairie also detail meticulously the number and burial place of the men killed in the action.

It was evident from the Mairie that the Commonwealth War Graves Commission take a close interest in the maintenance of the graves....there were a number of letters dating back to the twenties that warned the Mairie about dealing with weeds etc. The graves seemed meticulously looked after, that of John Norwood given colour by a dark red geranium. We drew to the attention of The War Graves Commission Headquarters in Brussels the mistakes made on the Sablonnieres village memorial and these were corrected. As for the cemetery, it remains very much part of the local community and locals tend their family graves alongside the fallen from a distant war.

John Norwood was the first VC to be killed in the Great War and his death therefore created something of a stir in that he was memorialised in the wartime edition of the Illustrated War News which recalled his Boer war exploits and reprinted the Melton Prior sketch that appeared in 1900 depicting his act of gallantry at Ladysmith. Lilian Norwood must have been devastated as she was left with three children to look after, the   9 year old John and the toddlers Robin and Diana. Moreover, her father General Sir Edwin Collen had died at Kelvedon in Essex in July 1911 leaving her mother alone; she died in 1935.The couple are buried together in the churchyard at Kelvedon in a grave beneath a vandalised, once - sturdy stone cross.

John left his wife well provided for - after probate, Lilian inherited over £30,000. She remained close to her brothers, two of whom went also to war, and is seen here with Edward Henry Ethelbert Collen whose path crossed with John's in both India and South Africa. Edward entered the war as a Major, was mentioned in Dispatches, and given the Brevet of Lieutenant Colonel 3 June, 1917. He was created a CMG in 1919. His brother Arthur George Pomeroy Collen entered the war as a Private but was soon commissioned and survived the war, leaving as a Major.

John left his medals to his sister Amy but when she died in 1926 within 24 hours of her husband, Ward Coldridge KC, they were left (together with the letter of command summoning John to Osborne to be decorated by Queen Victoria) to the young John. Amy gave Robin the original Melton Prior drawing and the safety pin used by Lord Roberts to pin the Victoria Cross on his father's chest in South Africa.

John Norwood's two sons attended Wellington and the young John was accepted at Cranwell as a cadet officer in 1925. He joined 23 Fighter Squadron in 1926 and then moved on in 1929 to Flight Instruction in which he was engaged for about 4 years at 5 Flight Training School Zeeland. He was posted in 1933 to 20 Squadron in Peshawar and then in 1935 to 28 Squadron in Chandigarh. He flew Audax biplanes in numerous displays of force and bombing sorties against dissident tribesmen on the Afghan frontier. This kind of activity had become almost a Collen-Norwood family tradition! In 1937 he attended Staff College at Andover after which he ceased to fly operationally. On the outbreak of

war, he had a series of major staff jobs with Fighter Command around the country until 1943 when again he followed his father to Southern Africa by taking up a Training command in Rhodesia. In 1944 he was involved in invasion planning in Cornwall and later served with Beaufighters in Scotland. His later years with the Airforce centred around Bomber Command and after a brief spell as Station Commander at RAF Khormaksar in Aden in 1948, he finally retired as a Group Captain in 1952. He married and had two children, Janet and Jillian who have had children of their own. He died in 1978.

Robin Norwood was interested in pursuing a military career but he was handicapped initially by a serious stammer. He became involved in various businesses including the sherry trade in Spain and then became a patent agent. He joined the Royal Air Force Volunteer Reserve well before the outbreak of war where his stammer did not seem to matter so much. He was trained on Spitfires in 1939 and was commissioned. In August 1940 he was posted to 65 Squadron in Hornchurch flying Spitfires and spent the next year engaged in defensive operations in the UK and cross channel attacks from a range of air stations including Turnhouse, St Andrews, Tangmere and Kirton Lindsey. He was detached for training duties in Hawarden and Uphaven from summer to autumn of 1941. His name appears on the Battle of Britain Memorials in London and Folkestone.

Robin joined 54 Squadron in 1942 and after sea sweeps from Thurso was posted in June to Australia via Capetown. His ultimate destination was Darwin where he was engaged in fierce fighting in 1943 against Japanese bomber raid operating from the Dutch Antilles and the Celebes against the Northern Territory. Many of his comrades died in these operations and also from operational accidents in Australia. They are commemorated in a plaque unveiled at the Darwin East Point Museum in 2014. Later, after the Japanese threat had receded, Robin spent a year or so in Australia as a ferry pilot before returning to the UK for a spell as instructor at the Air Gunnery School at RAF Walney in Cumbria with the rank of Flight

Lieutenant. He was then demobilised in 1946. He was regarded as a first class pilot by contemporaries known to the family and was able to control his stammer in the air.

Robin has three children, Gay, Martin and Richard. He turned to farming after the war which he continued until his death in 1970. His sons emigrated to Australia where they married and have brought up their own families. Alexander John Norwood and his cousin Linden, the great grandsons of John Norwood V.C. are the sole male descendants of that part of the Stilstead line of the Norwoods that passed through John Norwood VC. It is worth recalling at the end of this story that this pedigree stretches back to the marriage of Edith Swannaschels and King Harold Godwinson, whose reign came to a brutal end on the battlefield at Hastings in 1066.

 The last of John Norwood's children died in 2003, Diana Louise Norwood lived in Chelsea. Her apartment was not a stone's throw away from the house at 41 Oakley Street to which her father returned with such joy in 1900 to stay with his sister Amy after the lifting of the siege of Ladysmith. Diana was a radar operator during the Second World War and then moved to fighter control. Most of her life was spent working in the charity sector. She was a formidable and supportive aunt to the offspring of her brothers.

185

Norwood - Stilstead Line

Harold Godwinson - (King Harold) died 1066

Jordanus of Sheppey(Alnod)   1042-1126?
Sir Stephen de Northwood   b 1125
Sir Roger de Northwood - Lady Bona Fitzbernard d 1286.
Sir John de Northwood - Lady Joan de Badlesmere 1254-1319;
Sir John de Northwood - Lady Agnes de Grandison 1279- 1320
Sir Roger de Northwood - Margery de Halglton (widow) 1304-1361
Sir Roger de Northwood - Margaret de Halglton (step sister) 1323
Thomas de Northwood - Margaret de Montagu
Richard de Northwood 1374
Thomas Norwood   1395 - Joan de Berkeley b 1392.
Richard Norwood   1420-1485;
Richard Norwood   1450-1538 m Alice (1424 -1495)
Alexander Norwood d 1557; m Joan Howlett;
Alexander Norwood d 1583; m Joan Kemp d 1605
Manassas Norwood   1564 - 1636.
Richard Norwood m Anne Claybrooke 1618.
Paul Norwood   bpt 1629   m Jane Proude 1676.
Paul Norwood   1678-1724   m Mary Mass 1701.
Richard Norwood 1698-1775;   m Hannah Hatcher d. 1768)
John Norwood   1744-1816   m Sarah 1740-1820
Richard Norwood 1779-1841   m Elizabeth Barton.
Richard Norwood 1811 -1853   m Sarah E Booker 1837
John Norwood   1853- 1896   m Lucy Brown d 1890.
John Norwood VC 1876-1914   m Lilian Collen 1904

- John Norwood 1905-1978 m Griselda de la Rue
- Robin Norwood 1910-1970 m Dorothy Greenland
- Diana Norwood 1911- 2003